NUMEROLOGY MADE EASY

Published by
Melvin Powers
WILSHIRE BOOK COMPANY
12015 Sherman Road
No. Hollywood, California 91605
Telephone: (213) 875-1711

Printed by

HAL LEIGHTON PRINTING COMPANY
P.O. Box 3952
North Hollywood, California 91605
Telephone: (213) 983-1105

Printed in the United States of America
Library of Congress Catalog Card Number: 79-67148
ISBN 0-87980-376-2

CONTENTS

About the Author

Since his childhood days, William Mike has been naturally attracted to numbers. As his experience with numbers grew, he sensed a "link" between mathematics and philosophy, physics and metaphysics, numbers and language that would, he felt, open doors to new avenues of knowledge and understanding about ourselves and our world.

A graduate of Pennsylvania State University, Mr. Mike majored in both mathematics and philosophy. He continued his work in philosophy through post-graduate activity at California State University at Northridge. Additional classes at the University of California at Los Angeles have ranged from business and finance to public relations and writing. His metaphysical and spiritual studies have included the works of Joel S. Goldsmith, Swami Prabhavnanda, Edgar Cayce, Murdo Macdonald-Bayne, Corinne Helene, Catherine Ponder, Cheiro, Gerun More, C.W. Leadbeater, Dr. Joseph Murphy, Dr. Ervin Seale, Charles Filmore, Alice Bailey, Ernest Holmes and many more. It is from this direction that his widely diversified background and experience began to take shape. His activities have spanned the distance from business and financial counseling to Numerology to professional writing, lecturing and counseling.

Over the past fifteen years, Mr. Mike's career has included budget administration with the government, financial operations with Rockwell International and political consulting. He is the author of several magazine articles on Metaphysics, Meditation and Numerology.

Mr. Mike has developed a new and unique approach to the field of Numerology, not by chance, but by a lifetime of study and practice in the Language of Numbers. His seminars and lectures on this new method—which he calls *Numerolinguistics*—are popular throughout the West Coast.

Dedication

To Jessica
  Who always was, always is and always shall be—My Love.
To Cathy
  My child who can now follow the patterns of her own experiences.
To Indeia Anne
  Whose birth will give me continuous joy until she also flies free.

Introduction
Understanding the Language of Numbers

Numerology, the science of numbers, says that we have a set of numbers, that those numbers have meanings, and from those meanings we can find out our destiny, who we are compatible with, what our personality is really like and more.

Traditionally, books on Numerology have addressed only these individual aspects of our numbers—these separate parts—without showing us how these different aspects or parts relate to one without. Our numbers, however, define a sequence of events for us which, when taken in combination (as a whole, not as parts), describe the entire nature of our life experience. It is made up of the story which unfolds from the language of our numbers and their distinctive vibrational patterns. These "patterns" provide us with the blueprint for experiencing an exciting and fulfilling life.

This blueprint is personal and it is unique. With the language of numbers, there are ten basic aspects which define that blueprint. So, we find, the odds are *ten billion to one* that anyone else's blueprint will be the same as ours!

You can discover this architectural blueprint, this drawing, for it is available right now for you to read and to use. However, always remember that you are the one who supplies the variations on that blueprint, giving final shape to everything you may wish to experience. It indicates to you that you can succeed in a wide variety of arenas and all you have to do is prepare yourself for the action soon to be unfolding and awaiting your participation.

In order to expand your understanding of the basis of the language of numbers, I will be going into some of the supporting aspects of numbers. I will discuss the concept of the"Numero-log" (a diary of your personal numbers) and concentrate on the meaning and importance of *Compound Numbers*. Additional aspects include *Soul Qualities Development;* the value of *Compatibility Charts;* the importance of the interrelationship of the *four major aspects* of your blueprint; plus an overview of the nature of a *name change,* including why it is not as "crucially important" as you may have been led to believe.

When you develop your "set" of numbers and their corresponding definitions, what you will be seeing is a display of your own environmental patterns *as they unfold.* You will find yourself being able to tune in to what you are experiencing as you are experiencing it. Everyday of your life will be a totally new experience and a POSITIVE opportunity to enlarge your participation in it—whether you give conscious recognition to this fact or not.

Yes, even though the people, the events, places and situations now appear on the surface to be the same, you will discover that they *are* really in a constant process of change. And you can tune in and be part of this exciting change pattern, using it for your greatest benefit, if you but understand and utilize the language of your numbers.

1
The Language of Numbers
Numerology and Numerolinguistics

My whole premise in teaching Numerology, the science of numbers, was originally based on the simply stated fact that "everything doesn't just happen." It says that nothing happens by accident or chance, or at random. The more that I learned and understood about Numerology, the more I wanted to dispel the myths other "occultists" have perpetrated. These traditionalists always seem to emphasize the predictive or "mysterious" aspect of the information that comes from the numbers. It is time to start passing on all of the guidance available in these so-called occult sciences. They are only "occult" (mysterious, unrevealed) because of the human element in desiring to hide (except to a "chosen" few) what can easily be revealed.

Numerology has been around over 11,000 years, recognized at least since the beginning of recorded history. About 2,500 years ago, there was a Greek named Philolaus who said that Pythagoras (Greek mathematician, philosopher, spiritual leader) had supposedly developed a system of numbers that should be used in the "Western" world. And when I began my research and study in Numerology, I accepted this interpretation. However, I soon discovered that with the "Western" system, the interpretation of *birthname* numbers was not entirely accurate. The numbers of people's names were not reflecting who they really were.

The more I researched, the more I realized that the so-called "Western" Numerology was not on target. Had I paid more attention to the life and travels of Pythagoras, I would have known that he had studied under the

9

Jewish Mystics and the Gurus of India, had been "initiated" into many of the "mysteries" of the spiritual teachers of the East and had both used and taught *their* system of numbers. I took a longer and deeper look at the supposedly "different" systems and since the "schism" took place shortly after Pythagorus' death, I started my search there.

Pythagorus was a young man living in Asia Minor at the time when Cyrus the Great of Persia was creating a vast empire to the East. Cyrus was known as the "People's King," because he allowed freedom of travel, freedom in the arts, freedom of property and freedom of religion. I note the advent of Cyrus here, because it was the very nature of his Empire that allowed Pythagorus to travel throughout Cyrus' Empire and study under the mystics of Egypt, Chaldee, Judea and India.

It was not until Pythagorus was 60 years old that he founded a school to pass on the mystical sciences to Western students. This school was run by a religious brotherhood whose basis of belief was derived from mathematics, astronomy, physics and philosophy.

Pythagorus understood the nature of sound vibrations and the importance of numbers in the structure of science. There was never any evidence that he ever deviated from the teachings of the East which revealed to him the tools and techniques of the "mystery" schools.

A most unfortunate and disastrous occurrence took place near the end of Pythagorus' life. The people in the town where he founded his school became frightened of him and the "mysterious" knowledge he was passing on, so they destroyed his school and all of its records. As a result, very little of the teachings of Pythagorus survived.

One of the things which did survive was the story that Pythagorus deserted the Eastern system of Numerology and started the so-called "Western" system. This Western system, which not only discounted the validity of numerical vibrations, also seems to have somehow adapted itself to the "Anglo-Saxon" alphabet which was not even in existence at that time.

I suspect that one of his students, Philolaus by name, became a teacher under Pythagorus, and upon the death of Pythagorus wished to maintain credibility and authority in his dealings. Thus, in the name of his Master, he declared that a certain system of numbers (most probably his own) had been developed and blessed by Pythagorus.

Philolaus thereby set up Pythagorus as the Father of Western Numerology. And for 2,500 years, people have accepted this declaration when there has never been any evidence of its truth or validity.

I was one of those who initially accepted that truth until I learned about Chaldean Numerology. It is very closely related to the Vedic system of India and to the Qaballic system of the Jewish Mystics.

The Chaldean system is based on the fact that letters representing sound (phonetics) have vibrational patterns, that there are numbers which identify their vibrational patterns. These patterns are then translated into a language which can be understood and used by everyone. This language provides you a blueprint of potential choices from the numbers of your name at birth and from the numbers of your birthdate.

The major difference between the Chaldean and Western systems is the alphabet/number designation of each system. The Chaldean system assigns the number value by *sound*. The Western system assigns the number value by the sequence of the Western alphabet, a equals 1, b equals 2, c equals 3, d equals 4, e equals 5, f equals 6, g equals 7, h equals 8, and i equals 9. The number assignment of the Western system would then repeat itself down the alphabet, starting with the 1 again and proceeding through the #9, continuing to repeat the sequence until the letter z.

However, the Western alphabet assignment, totally discounts the most important aspect of Numerology—the concept of vibration and the numerical designation of each vibrational pattern. As a result, the Western system virtually destroys the validity of birthname numbers (or any other name number) and their meaning.

Most current Numerology books pay only lip service to the interpretation of names, with the main emphasis on how easily one can change their name. Obviously, we can change our names anytime we choose. But that misses the "point" about our birthnames. What Western numerology fails to acknowledge is the fact that the language of the numbers of our names at birth gives us the *most* important facts about the direction in which our lives are unfolding.

The point is that patterns of our names at birth, in conjunction with the patterns of our birthday vibratory force become the basis for focusing in on our life's blueprint of experiences. The only way for focusing in on our life's blueprint is to understand the language behind our numbers. It is a process of interpretation that I call *Numerolinguistics.*

Numerolinguistics is the study of the nature and structure of the language of numbers. While Numerology derives its validity from the nature of sound vibrations of letters with number values identified, Numerolinguistics translates the vibrational behavior of the numbers into written symbols and meaningful patterns.

These symbols and patterns describe the specific influences, unfolding environmental possibilities (potential environments or situations) and potential events of each vibrational focal point (identified by number). In other words, we can be shown a blueprint of the model of our life experiences, an unfolding scenario that can be likened to the patterns on a lake that take form when a stone strikes the water causing a series of concentric circles to move out from the point of contact.

The vibrational patterns give one a distinct view of the direction or "unfoldment" of their own life experiences, helping in making decisions, in supplying variations, and in taking right action. These symbols, patterns, environmental possibilities and events are part of a "blueprint" from which we, as architects of our own lives, can build or develop our life experiences. Knowing our vibrational blueprint permits us to become *consciously aware* of those available "natural" aspects which we can choose to help us focus on *OUR* own unique *path* toward a fulfilling life. In so doing, we can learn to "resonate" to the inner vibrations that are constantly flowing outward from the center of our being toward our environment. You can use "Numerolinguistics" and the language of numbers as a process to move from where you are to where you want to be, you can use it for your own amazement and enjoyment or you can use it in working with others.

2
Your Purpose in Life Revealed
The Numbers of Your Full Name at Birth

Understanding the language of your numbers can show you how to get in tune with the major events taking place in your life, what action to take, which doors to enter and why. You will be able to give yourself your "own" advice and not have to depend on others for guidance and counseling. This understanding will allow you to bring out the best of "you", to give equal recognition to all of your aspects, and to express all of your talent and ability.

You will be able to let your intuition work for you as an equal partner with your intellect. You will discover the natural expression of your emotions and why you feel the way you do. And you will be better able to get in tune with your physical environment. As strange as it may seem, all of these things can be shown to you from the numbers of your name at birth and your birthdate.

There are four major aspects of your numbers which are the foundation stones upon which the "house" of your life experiences is built. These four aspects can provide you the blueprint of the unfolding patterns of your life. Your name at birth has within its numbers *three* of these major aspects. The language of the numbers of your birthname can give you very important and useful information about yourself and your environment.

The most important aspect of your birthname is revealed by the numbers of your *full name at birth* Whatever name is on your *birth certifi-*

cate is the one that counts, whether your mother decided to change your name because she didn't like the one your father gave you, whether your father forced your mother to change it at the last minute, or whether the doctor or nurse made an error in spelling. For what is *finally* placed on the birth certificate defines the nature of the vibrational patterns that are you.

Your full birthname is the name identity by which you are *called* at birth. It is your *Purpose* and it is your *Mission* and the way you are to express in the world.

(NOTE: To find the numbers of your full name at birth, see the instructions below and Illustration 2a.)

I call this "Purpose" your intuitive perspective, that view of your life experiences which says this is what you *should* be to gain the most from living. It is that perspective which your other aspects may not be aware of to any degree. Its source is from your inner "beingness" (soul, higher self, essence), the part of your total expression which gives you intuitive knowing, or "hunches".

This intuitional aspect within you is that part of you which "watches" your physical, emotional and intellectual aspects in operation. However, it is, for the most part, left out of one's experiencing, particularly by the male of the species. Men always seem to be quite intent on·giving their intellectual perspective dominance. This intellectual aspect is discussed in more depth in Chapter 5.

There is a blueprint of your life's experiences. There are certain general things which you will do, certain growth which you will experience and certain value which you will pull from these experiences. The intuitive aspect is the part of you that knows about those things before you become aware of them. It is the link between your experiencing (physical, emotional and intellectual) and what has been called the Superconscious Mind.

Your "Purpose" is only the minimum of what you can achieve and is what your "higher" self wants you to be, urges you to be, but *only if you choose* to accomplish it. It is that particular way in which you can experience your world and find your greatest satisfaction and fulfillment in it.

To find the number of your full name at birth (your Purpose), you first lay out the letters of your name on a sheet of paper such that you will have room to place numbers underneath each letter of your name. (see illustration 2a). Now, using the Chaldean alphabet/number assignment, assign the correct number value to the letters of your name.

Add the numbers of your first name together and place the sum below the first name. If the sum is a compound number (two or more digits), then add the compound numbers until you have a single digit (i.e., if the total equals 26, then add 2 plus 6 to equal 8).

Then, add the numbers of your middle name (assuming you have one) until the final total is a single digit.

Finally, add the numbers of your last name until you have a single digit. (NOTE: In all cases, if the initial sum of any of the names is an *11* or a *22* then DO NOT reduce to a single digit.)

Now, add the number of the first name to the number of the middle name to the number of the last name. If the total is a compound number, then reduce it to a single digit unless it is an *11* or *22*, which are MASTER numbers and have specific significance.

The name that you go by, accept and/or use, happens to reflect the vibrational patterns of the role that you are playing, or an event or situation you are experiencing. You attract the name that fits the experience. Normally, the "names" that you are called or like to be called are sounds that you like or feel comfortable with. As a result, you "bring" certain environmental patterns into your experiencing, or *image* certain models of living that you have built up inside your mind.

What about those people who literally cannot stand their birthnames? When you resent or hate your birthname, it is indicative of your rebellion against the particular blueprint outlined for you. You're unconsciously rebelling against the unfolding vibrational patterns which you (your higher self) had purposely planned for your own experiencing.

This creates conflict in your view of life and in your values or concepts of living. It normally shows up in a dissatisfied lifestyle; a dissatisfaction with your career; an indifference as to what happens to you; or a failure to develop close or lasting relationships with people. Although you may be aware of the rebellion or conflict, you may not be aware of the root cause of your dissatisfaction.

However, it doesn't really matter what name you use. What is important is that *you experience that which is in tune with what you are.* The vibrational patterns of your name give you valuable and valid knowledge about who and what you are. When someone says to you, "Be what and who you are," you no longer have to ask "How do I know that?" or "How do I find out?" Now, you have a way of getting in touch with who and what you are, without uncertainty, without the need for some self-awareness workshops or self-image course of instruction. It doesn't matter what you are called, as long as you are in tune with the truth of your own being, know who and what you are, and are aware of and take advantage of the experiences that come to you. These vibrational patterns will develop as the experiences of your life express naturally.

ILLUSTRATION 2a

PURPOSE, MISSION, WORLD EXPRESSION

Finding the Number of Your Birthname

Chaldean Alphabet/Number System*

1 2 3 4 5 6 7 8

A B C D E U O F
I K G M H V Z P
J R L T N W
Q S X
Y

BIRTHNAME: W I L L I A M   P H I L L I P   M I K E

ALPHABET/NUMBERS: 6 1 3 3 1 1 4   8 5 1 3 3 1 8   4 1 2 5

**

WILLIAM: $6 + 1 + 3 + 3 + 1 + 1 + 4 = 19 = 1 + 9 = 10 = 1 + 0$ $= \underline{1}$

$+$ $+$

PHILLIP: $8 + 5 + 1 + 3 + 3 + 1 + 8 = 29 = 2 + 9 = 11$ $= \underline{11}$

$+$ $+$

MIKE: $4 + 1 + 2 + 5 \quad = 12 = 1 + 2 = 3$ $= \underline{3}$

                                                               **
                                                               15

Total Birthname Number $= 1 + 11 + 3 = 15 = 1 + 5 = \underline{6}$

---

* The Chaldean/Vedic/Qaballic systems did not assign the #9 to any letter. In the ancient "mystery" schools of knowledge, the #9 was considered the most "sacred" of numbers. Its vibratory force included the attributes of all the numbers and, therefore, did not (could not) represent any individual symbol or letter.

** See Chapter 10 for Compound Number meanings.

Birthname Number

The Number	The Description

1

The keynote of the #1 is "the inherent right" of the *individual* to be themselves.

You must face and pass the test of *originality/action/independence;* you must succeed through your own efforts.

Your accomplishments come through the drive of your free will, self reliance, and your own ability.

Show courage/valor/initiative, for you will be looked to for strength and force of character; be aware to control any tendency to selfishness, overlooking group aims.

You will be given opportunities to help others discover their "individuality."

You are a natural executive, leader, pioneer and promoter.

2

Your key to success is by working in association with others, not by competing.

You can be a diplomat, peacemaker, harmonizer, mediator; to establish peace, balance, and harmony, for you can see both sides of the issues.

A good sense of timing, rhythm and color are yours.

Your psychic abilities are inherent; you have great insight to the feelings of others.

Sharing and partnership are the best approach in experiencing your environment; you would make a good companion.

Cooperation and tactfulness are your bywords.

You have patience in handling details and compiling materials for future use.

3

You have within you the natural ability of expressing a vivid and creative imagination.

You are to arouse spirit and imagination so that others

The Number	The Description

may learn how to experience the lighter, more joyful side of life.

Be careful not to scatter your talents; complete one pursuit before moving on or you may not accomplish anything substantive.

You have a gift of words that will allow you to achieve through writing, acting or speaking.

You can find success in the theater, opera, literature, writing, as a society leader or organizer.

4

The #4 is the symbol of foundation, framework, and the square as put to use by the carpenter.

You are a builder; your joy and fulfillment come through hard work and determination.

The ideals of honesty, equality and straightforwardness are of second nature to you; you can help others by passing on your understanding to them.

You should be disciplined, analytical, systematic and practical.

You can succeed as a mason, contractor or instructor; you are an organizer, manager and supervisor.

Your inherent abilities will make you reliable, dependable and efficient.

5

Yours should be a life of action, with many and varied experiences.

You are a natural traveller.

You should experience freedom and liberty.

Learn that change means progress *not* uncertainty; that change means growth and expansion; and as you learn, pass that understanding on to those around you.

"Spread the Word" of freedom—not only freedom from restrictions, limitations, taboos, but also freedom born of the act of creative expression.

The Number	The Description

You can find success in writing, speaking, communications, public relations.

You are versatile, clever and courageous.

6 — "Doing unto others as you would have them do unto you," keynotes the pattern of your experiences.

You can be the "cosmic" parent or teacher in service to home and community; and to work from a position of great responsibility and trust.

Since harmony, rhythm, love and beauty are paramount in your life, music and theater arts would be natural for you.

You will be a strong influence in establishing harmony and beauty in every environment where you abide.

You are a great inspiration to people when you express the finer side of your nature.

7 — You can excel as an "educator" in the field of science (physics, chemistry, or engineering) or meta-science (metaphysics and the spiritual sciences).

You are a deep thinker and need to spend time alone and in silence.

Don't live by superficialities; be a specialist, a realist.

Learn to see the reality behind the appearance by gaining understanding, wisdom and discrimination.

Learn the difference between the real and the illusory.

Partnerships may not be successful for you unless you work at it.

You have an innate sympathy, a sensitive nature, inner power and substance.

You can be a "healer" of the body, the mind and the emotions.

8 — Power, organization and the executive ability are natural to you; you are a natural director.

You are to learn of the relationship between material and spiritual power and to pass that learning on.

Make an efort to acquire money and position and to share with loved ones and those in need; develop breadth of outlook and admit no limitation.

Your watchwords are justice, mercy and judgment (as of "Solomon").

Success comes through your own efforts, not luck.

Don't let any failures discourage you (they're only temporary); deserting your purpose or ideals will bring you unhappiness.

Your sharp sense of judgment can bring you success in a court of law or in business and finance.

9   Bywords of the #9 are compassion, tolerance, understanding and service.

You can achieve success as a spiritual leader, teacher, healer or as a philanthropist.

Success as a writer/lecturer in humanitarian/spiritual arena emphasized.

Learn to give freely of emotions through inspiration, kindness and understanding.

Develop impersonality (not indifference) and an objective view of experiencing; taking things too personally or too seriously could bring you unnecessary pain.

You may face unwanted sacrifices; face them' and resolve them; to withdraw may bring unhappiness that comes from leaving things undone.

11   The #11 is a *Master* number and lifts the #2 to limelight activities.

You can be a Super Diplomat, Super Mediator, Super Peacemaker.

You can succeed as an Evangelist, Minister, Reformer or as a psychologist or psychoanalyst.

The Number	The Description
	This vibration is "magnetic," and indicates an "electrical" individual with originality and intuition. You are an inspirational visionary; learn to express your ideals so that you can pass on the "truths" that you see. Natural areas for you exist in the field of electricity, including TV and Radio (either in front or behind the scenes making things work). Number elevens are generally called to action for some great cause; not all respond—being satisfied with fulfillment as a #2.
22	The #22 is also a *Master* number and represents the "Master Builder" as well as being the number of Super Statesman. It is the number of international fame and activity. You have the potential to open up new fields and to build the roads on which others will follow toward goals you have defined and for which you have already set the groundwork. Where the #4 lays the foundation or builds the framework for their home or community, the #22 does it for the world. The 22 raises the vibration of the 4 to use the inherent abilities of the 4 in working with large groups and assuming great responsibilities.

3
Finding Your
Heart's Desire
The Vowels of Your Birthname

Your vowels are the reflection of your emotions, the way you feel about things, people, places and situations. The language of the numbers behind the *vowels* of your name at birth gives you a blueprint of *how* you will feel about your life, your experiences, the people you meet, the things you do, the events in which you participate, and your environment.

The nearest thing to defining the nature of your vowels would be the *desires of your heart*. Your vowels give you what I call your emotional perspective, clues to knowing why you feel the way you do about important aspects of your experiences.

(NOTE: To find the "number" of your vowels, see the method described below and Illustration 3a.)

The blueprint given to you at birth shows you certain key things: it shows you what seeds have been planted, how they may grow and what they can produce for you. The seeds of your emotional experiences are planted in the patterns of your vowels. They express the emotional view that unfolds in your life.

The language of your vowels can also be said to reflect the "inner you," the way you view yourself and your life. But it is only a partial picture influenced by what you have experienced. You develop certain models which you worship and swear by, models of things which you want to bring into your life, models of jobs, places and people which you feel are right for you. Your emotions "react" to the environment in which you find yourself based on the models you have established on that inner level.

You can know which basic environment "feels" the best for you or the one in which you would feel best through the language of the "number" of your vowels. This "inner you", your psychological being, is that part of you which interprets and expresses your emotional responses to the people and environment around you.

To find the "number" of your vowels, lay out your full name at birth on a sheet of paper with room to place numbers below the letters. Then, under the *vowels only*, put the correct number value under each vowel (See the Chaldean alphabet/number assignment in Illustration 3a.)

Add the numbers of the vowels of your first name together and reduce to a single digit, *except if they add to an 11* or *22* which are MASTER numbers (with a special meaning) and are not to be reduced further. Add the numbers of the vowels of your middle name (assuming you have one) in the same manner as the first name. Then add the numbers of your last name.

Finally, add the vowel numbers of each name together to find the "*number*" of your vowels. Reduce to a single digit *unless* it is an *11* or *22*. Now read the "numbers" definitions at the end of this chapter.

The urge to go somewhere important or to do something major is almost invariably tied to the language of the numbers of your vowels and their descriptive patterns. Your vowels will confirm your dreams and reflect the desires of your heart.

ILLUSTRATION 3a

HEART'S DESIRE, INNER YOU

Finding the Number of Your Vowels

Chaldean Alphabet/Number System*

1 2 3 4 5 6 7 8

A B C D E U O F
I K G M H V Z P
J R L T N W
Q S X
Y

BIRTHNAME: W I L L I A M   P H I L L I P   M I K E
(Vowels Underlined)

ALPHABET/NUMBERS: 1   1 1   1   1   1   5

WILLIAM   = 1 + 1 + 1 =   3
    +   +
PHILLIP   = 1 + 1   =   2
    +   +
MIKE   = 1 + 5   =   6
                       ——————
                          **
Your Vowel Number   = 3 + 2 + 6 = 11

* The Chaldean/Vedic/Qaballic systems did not assign the #9 to any letter. In the ancient "mystery" schools of knowledge, the #9 was considered the most "sacred" of numbers. Its vibratory force included the attributes of all numbers and, therefore, did not (could not) represent any individual symbol.

** See Chapter 10 for Compound Number meanings.

HEART'S DESIRE, INNER YOU
The Numbers of Your Vowels

The Number	The Description
1	Inherent in this vibration is the desire to be at the front of life's parade; to lead and direct others or their activities, not to be subordinate to events and/or people.

The
Description

You have the ability to operate from the strength and courage of your convictions.

Watch the desire to dominate any situation; overdoing it may work to your detriment.

Beware of impressions of arrogance which can cause unpleasant reactions from others.

Learn to cultivate diplomacy, patience and tact.

Be creative and original; you are a "pioneer" of new things.

2

Friendliness is your byword; you seek the comfort of companionship and camaraderie.

Diplomacy and tactfulness are natural to you; you can see yourself as an arbiter or peacemaker.

The keynote of the #2 is cooperation, kindness and thoughtfulness.

You are sensitive and emotional; you are not fond of display or aggressiveness and you may be "too" easy going for your own good.

You may prefer the background to being upfront.

Your psychic ability is latent and very close to the surface. This ability can be developed very quickly if you desire it.

Your success can be enhanced, if you develop discipline and a definite purpose.

3

You have the innate talent to express yourself creatively in *words*—writing, speaking, singing or acting.

You desire beauty and laughter in your environment.

You can find great pleasure by learning to express your thoughts and imagination in a lighter vein.

You are a "natural" entertainer—whether in front of friends, large groups or in public.

Seek knowledge, ambition and independence.

Cultivate tolerance, patience and concentration.

The Number	The Description
	Watch any tendency to scatter talents.
4	Things practical, analytical, methodical, orderly and reliable appeal to you.
	Bywords include loyalty, discipline, determination and detail.
	You may dislike things that are unfinished or incorrect.
	Manual dexterity may be evident with an affinity to carpentry, pottery, mechanics or metalwork; you can take and follow instructions to the letter.
	Respectability, stability and dependability are important to you.
	You may react unfavorably to change and innovation; learn how to discard things no longer useful or valid; be careful not to be narrow-minded in your viewpoint; cultivate a broader view.
5	For this #5 vibration, variety is "indeed" the spice of life.
	You may have a very strong urge for travel and adventure.
	The keynote is that everyone's heritage is the "right" of personal freedom in all directions.
	Change, movement, action and versatility are your bywords, as you search for "freedom."
	You are naturally clever, witty and curious.
	You should find yourself leaning towards things that are investigative and promotive, spurred on by the dislike of routine, detail and conformity.
	Cultivate concentration.
6	The foundation stones of the #6 are love, truth, beauty and justice.
	It is keynoted by service to others—as teacher, counselor, parent and friend—as a humanitarian.

The Number	The Description

You desire to feel and know love on a personal as well as on a universal level of awareness.

Love and the need of a home and family environment (a home base, roots) are essential to you.

Ease, comfort and artistic recognition are important to you.

Great success can be yours when you learn to balance your feelings and thinking, your intellect and emotions.

7

You are introspective, intellectual, philosophical and spiritual.

You are a natural in the study of the unknown, whether physical or metaphysical.

Your intuition is finely tuned, and it can be said that you have an "illumined intellect".

You are highly analytical and consider all angles; you are sometimes "too much" the perfectionist.

Intellectual courage is held in high esteem for you.

You are deeply emotional but afraid to show it; you have the ability to inspire, but reluctantly use it.

Learn to overcome the tendency to be reserved, conservative, and withdrawn.

8

You respect power and success.

You see power, acclaim and authority as a means to get "quality" from life.

You should become involved in large operations—especially in the financial/commercial world.

The ability to work very hard to achieve your goals is instinctual for you; you dislike laziness and second best.

You have good judgement and an excellent sense of values; you have strength, enthusiasm, power, determination and efficiency.

You can find great success as a business executive, leader or manager.

The Number	The Description
	You have an expansive viewpoint and are generous and dependable.
	Develop the willpower to organize, cooperate and move ahead.
9	You want to be a humanitarian and be of service to the world—a "UNIVERSAL SISTER/BROTHER".
	You have a deep desire and need for personal love, but you belong to the universe; be aware of your emotions so that you do not suffer through them; your pain will come if you take things, people or events "too" personally.
	You give freely of yourself without thoughts of your own discomfort.
	You have boundless faith in your own unending source of supply and energy.
	You love and appreciate the arts, dramatics and music.
	Wisdom, intuition and a broad viewpoint are yours.
11	This *MASTER* number is both intuitional and inspirational, with the continual desire to reveal the vision of beauty that is available to everyone.
	Your psychic ability is inborn; you could be a "seer" or a "counselor".
	You are inventive with an electrical type of mind.
	You will always have the urge to be in the public limelight passing on truth.
	Since the #11 is the dreamer or the visionary, you must be careful not to love ideals more than people.
	To become the Super Diplomat and Peacemaker that you can become, you must cultivate "human" understanding.
	You have greater interior strength and can carry great responsibilities.
22	The "22" vibration stands for the "ideal realized."

You can be a MASTER BUILDER (for eternity); you continually strive for perfection.

Develop the spiritual and idealistic "POWER" that is yours to use.

You have the ability to make useful and practical things magnificent and uplifting.

You need to continuously cultivate a steadfast adherence to your ideals in the midst of materiality or conflict.

Mingle with the public and give knowledge to everyone.

4
Your Personality Profile
The Consonants of Your Birthname

The third major aspect of your name at birth is understood through the *consonants* of your birthname. This aspect addresses the "physical" perspective which you display and also refers to the physical environment which you experience through your five senses of taste, touch, sight, sound and smell. And it is the physical appearance or impression you make in your environment. It is the outer you, as others see you—it is your *personality*.

Where your full name at birth shows your *intuitive* response to your life and the vowels your *emotional* response, your consonants define your *physical* response. The language of your consonants can provide you with clues as to the kind of clothes you would look best in, to the style of car which would appeal to you, to how you see others and how others see you. Your consonants can give you some insight into understanding the nature of your "physical" relationships.

(NOTE: To find the "number" of your consonants see the method below and the Illustration 4a.)

When you walk into a room full of people, you will certainly make a "first" impression. You give off specific "vibrations" which people pick up and interpret, and you don't even have to speak a single word! People tune in first to the "outer" you which goes "before" you to make a "first" impression.

How many times have you seen someone and said, "I know where they're coming from!'' or "I know that type!''? And how many times have you heard people say they always go with their first impression, that the first impression is always right? When people view things this way, they are only dealing with the outer surface or superficial aspect of others. If you do not care about knowing the essence of a person, if you do not go beyond the surface contact, your first impression would, of course, always be "right".

Through the language of your consonants you can discover why people react to you differently than you might expect or think they should. It will also allow you to stop and reconsider first impressions you may get, so that you can find out, then and there, whether your first impression is the "right" one.

To find the "number" of your consonants, lay out your full name at birth on a sheet of paper with room to place numbers underneath the letters. Then, under the *consonants only*, put the correct number value under each consonant (see the Chaldean alphabet/number assignment in Illustration 4a.)

Add the numbers of the consonants of your first name together and reduce to a single digit, unless they are the *11* or *22* which are the MASTER numbers (with a special meaning) and are not to be reduced further. Add the numbers of the consonants of your middle name in the same manner. Then add the numbers of the consonants of your last name.

Finally, add the consonant numbers of each name together to find the *"number"* of your consonants. Reduce to a single digit *unless* it is the *11* or *22*. Now, read the number definitions displayed at the end of this chapter.

"Could it only be that God would give us the gift to see ourselves as others see us," wrote Chaucer.

Understanding the language of the numbers of your consonants can give you exactly that—the gift to see yourself as others see you.

ILLUSTRATION 4a

PERSONALITY, AS OTHERS SEE YOU

Finding the Number of Your Consonants

Chaldean Alphabet/Number System*

1 2 3 4 5 6 7 8

A B C D E U O F
I K G M H V Z P
J R L T N W
Q S X
Y

BIRTHNAME: W I L L I A M P H I L L I P M I K E

ALPHABET/NUMBERS: 6 3 3 4 8 5 3 3 8 4 2

WILLIAM: 6 + 3 + 4 = 16 = 7
+   +
PHILLIP: 8 + 5 + 3 + 3 + 8 = 27 = 9
+   +
MIKE: 4 + 2 = 6 = 6
                                        **
Your Consonant Number = 7 + 9 + 6 = 22

* The Chaldean/Vedic/Qaballic systems did not assign the #9 to any letter. In the ancient "mystery" schools of knowledge, the #9 was considered the most "sacred" of numbers. Its vibratory force included the attributes of all numbers and, therefore, did not (could not) represent any individual symbol or letter.

** See Chapter 10 for Compound Number meanings.

PERSONALITY, AS OTHERS SEE YOU
The Numbers of Your Consonants

The Number	The Description
1	The #1 can be seen as courageous and daring, or self indulgent and selfish.

The Number	The Description
	Many will react to you as a "leader" or as a promoter of new enterprises.
	Many will see you as dominant, forceful, as well as creative.
2	You are seen as neat, clean, pleasing and agreeable.
	You give off an aura of peace, quiet and diplomacy.
	You send out vibrations of "cooperation" and the "willingness to help others."
	Many will see you as harmonious and unobtrusive.
3	You may be seen as expressive, talkative, friendly, sociable and popular.
	Vibrations of success, ambition and authority flow from you; you may tend to draw enemies who are jealous of your success or "apparent" success.
	You have a strong willpower and sense of determination.
	Many see you as having no worries or concerns.
4	You are seen by others as practical, dependable, stable, disciplined and a "hard worker" who always seems to have your "nose to the grindstone."
	You give the impression of being conservative, orderly and self reliant.
	You are a tower of strength, and may have "square" shoulders.
5	You are seen as a seeker of adventure, versatile, carefree and fearless.
	You build for present happiness.
	You are gracious, magnetic and interesting.
	Good imagination, good sense of humor and good conversation are attributes of your personality.

The Number	The Description
6	You enjoy the "quiet" of meditation and contemplation.
	You are seen by many as having it all together (harmonious).
	You are neat, attractive and sympathetic.
	Others seek you out for advice and comfort.
7	The #7 personality is one that appears to be quiet, relaxed and attracted to solitude and peace.
	You are seen as having intelligence and wisdom.
	Many consider you subtle, elusive, aloof, reserved and exclusive.
	You are also seen as "well-groomed."
8	You dislike cheap things or being second best.
	You know how to deal with material and business problems you face.
	You are seen as friendly, persuasive and dominant.
	You admire success and have the ambition to achieve.
	Your personality is seen as well-balanced and efficient.
	You give the impression of power and authority.
9	You are seen as sincere, well-balanced, truthful and noble.
	You are a magnetic personality, but sometimes lack the force of follow-through in developing friendships.
	You are seen as a "big brother"/"big sister," generous and sympathetic.
	You consider yourself a romantic and feel you are working in the service of mankind.
11	You are seen as a dreamer with your head in the clouds.
	You are idealistic, spiritual and inspirational.

The Number	The Description

You may see yourself as a martyr (in the name of faith and glory).

Many see you as a bearer of truth.

Your personality is individualistic and electrical in its actions.

22

You are seen as either a "know-it-all," an expert or a master builder.

You are seen by many as being extremely practical with your feet firmly planted on the ground.

Even when you are broke, you give off the appearance of wealth.

Many believe that you can make dreams come true.

5
The Shape of
Your Destiny
The Numbers of Your Birthdate

Your birthdate number reveals the nature of your *thinking* process and the fields of knowledge and endeavor to which your thinking will lead you. It gives you your *intellectual* perspective, what you *think* you should be to experience life fully. It is the way your intellect "looks" at the how, what, when, where and why of your experiences.

Your birthdate number is known as the number of your Destiny, the number of your life cycle or path which defines the nature of your personal reality. Your mind is the center for controlling and initiating action. Your Destiny Number refers to your ability to create your own environment or shape your own career. It refers to the fact that everything around you in this world is perceived or sensed through the interpretation which your mind gives you (as influenced by your emotional reactions and prejudices, of course).

Your mind provides the discipline (or fails to). Your mind is responsible for your ultimate choice of things, for your judgments and for your decisions. It is the instrument which shapes your life and molds your environment, your individual reality of experiencing, your *Destiny*.

(NOTE: The method for finding your Destiny Number is shown below and in Illustration 5a.).

Most people identify more with the language of their Destiny Number (intellect) than to the language of their names at birth (intuitive perspective). You always pay attention to your birthdate number, since it is celebrated year after year. You are usually less in tune with the vibrational patterns of your birthname numbers since your birthname has been "changed" (i.e. "nicknames") almost from the first day you were born. In the beginning, others change it for you; later, you change your name yourself to "fit" your environment.

When you change your name, or are given a "new" one, the vibrational patterns which unfold around you fit a specific role you are playing or a new situation that you are in. However, your Destiny Number (birthdate) never changes, and is very strongly tied to the way you think about your life, your experiences, and things in general.

It is interesting to note that when our "mind" is made up, how difficult it is to change it, but that our feelings, hunches, and physical tastes (shown in the patterns of our name) change constantly and sometimes *very* quickly.

The four most important numbers (basic aspects) of your blueprint are your Purpose (intuition), Heart's Desire (emotion), Personality (physical) and Destiny (intellect). The first three key off of your birthname, while your Destiny and all other important aspects key off of your birthdate. The only exception to this is your Goal Power or Final Opportunity Number which is determined by adding togther your Purpose Number (intuition) to your Destiny Number (intellect). This defines the path of greatest success, during the last half of your life, achieved through the "integration" of your intuition and intellect (see Chapter 6).

To find the number of your Destiny, write out your birthdate on a sheet of paper and calculate its number by adding the number of the month to the number of the day to the number of the year (see Illustration 5a).

If your birthday were September 21, 1938, the number of the month is *9.* The number of the day (21) is 2 plus 1 equals *3.* The number of the year is found by adding its digits together. 1 plus 9 plus 3 plus 8 equals 21 which becomes 2 plus 1 equals *3.* Now add each of these numbers together—*9* plus *3* plus *3* equals *15,* which when reduced to a single digit, becomes *1* plus 5 equals 6. This number 6 would be the number of your destiny. Its patterns are defined at the end of this chapter.

The number 1 Destiny vibrational pattern is indeed "Numero Uno": stage center, up front, a leader not a follower. The number 2 excels as a follower. The bywords of the number 2 are cooperation, diplomacy, graciousness, mediation and support. The number 3 is the entertainer, the number of the creative and performing arts and self expression. Solidarity symbolizes the number 4, the four corners, the square. It is the number of method detail, logic, and dependability. The number 5 likes change, action, movement, variety, words, communication and travel. It represents words in action.

The number 6 represents trust, responsibility, harmony, balance and truth. It is the number of the teacher, parent, counselor and advisor. The number 7 is mystical in nature and seeks to lift the "veil" of mystery from life. The 7 can be a scientist, both physical and metaphysical. The Cosmic Organizer flows from the pattern of the 8 destiny. It brings with it super-intuition, judgment, authority and executive ability. The number 9 is the number of healing, protection, energy and metaphysics and universality. Its bywords are service (to humanity), compassion and objectivity.

Remember you cannot look at these descriptions isolating them individually, and do justice to understanding the language of your numbers. Always look at all your numbers as parts of a whole.

Whether or not you are consciously aware of it, your mind is active during two-thirds of your life, perceiving, receiving, judging, deciding. The unfolding patterns of your Destiny Number have a decided impact on the way that you "think" about your experiences. The language of your birthdate number defines your intellectual process and shows you what you can achieve through the *power of your mind*. Understanding that language can aid you in fulfilling that Destiny.

ILLUSTRATION 5a.

DESTINY, LIFE PATH, REALITY CYCLE

Finding the Numbers of Your Birthdate

UNIVERSAL (Calendar) MONTH NUMBERS

January	=	1	July	=	7
February	=	2	August	=	8
March	=	3	September	=	9
April	=	4	October	=	1
May	=	5	November	=	2
June	=	6	December	=	3

BIRTHDATE: September   21,   1938
$$9 \qquad 3 \qquad 1 + 9 + 3 + 8$$
$$9 \qquad 3 \qquad 21$$
$$9 \qquad 3 \qquad 2 + 1$$
$$9 \ + \ 3 \ + \ 3 \ = \ 15*$$
BIRTHDATE NUMBER $= 15 = 1 + 5 = \underline{6}$

* See Chapter 10 for Compound Number meanings.

DESTINY, LIFE PATH, REALITY CYCLE
Birthdate Numbers

The Number	The Description
1	Numero Uno, the "innovator," the leader; a strong "individual-oriented" vibrational pattern.
	Originality, creativity, ambition are inherent.
	Executive ability, strength and willpower are inbred in the number one's nature.
	A positive, generous nature predominates.
	You were meant to be in the driver's seat, not a passenger or follower.
	Watch the tendency to be domineering and hasty, headstrong, and bossy; it could be detrimental to your success. Learn to use diplomacy.
2	The "Diplomat," the "Peacemaker."
	Keynoted by natural tact, courtesy, cooperation and agreeability.

The Number	The Description

Your greatest success comes through a supportive role, helping someone develop their plans or expand their ideas.

You have a natural graciousness and consideration of others.

This is the number of "receptivity"—receiving good through your cooperative spirit, not needing to aggressively "go after" anything.

You have the ablity to bring life and form to many things.

An innate sense of rhythm and timing are yours.

You have the potential ability to see both sides of issues, to settle disputes and to mediate.

3   A number 3 can very easily become known as "The Entertainer."

You have the gift of words and a "quick" sense of humor.

You are mental (intuitive), versatile and have the ability to gain knowledge quickly.

You have no difficulty making friends.

Areas of success include critic, writer, speaker or singer.

Guard against being too critical of others, too impatient and too intolerant.

Don't scatter talents; use them or success could be dampened.

Learn to give of your talents freely.

Love is a necessity with you on a "real" sharing basis.

4   The number of the "CARPENTER"; the building of a foundation.

The symbol of the square and discipline.

This represents the "down-to-earth" aspects of life and gives you a sense of form and structure.

The Number	The Description

Your life will be one of work, dedication, duty, justice and equality.

Keywords are patience, endeavor, method, detail and dependability.

Be careful not to be "too" set in your ways; it may be detrimental to your success.

5

Freedom is your password through life, highlighted by change, variety, travel and the unexpected.

Learn the *right* use of freedom; constantly seek the new and untried and profit from them by understanding all classes and conditions of people.

You are a "reporter"; a natural in the use of WORDS (lecturing, writing, selling, investigating).

Do not remain in a rut; learn the lesson of "discard."

Enjoy all of the action that unfolds around you.

6

Learn the meaning of responsibility, and how to balance opposites.

The number 6 is the number of the "Cosmic Parent," teacher of high ideals, and counselor.

Seek to keep the scales of justice in balance.

You are destined to be of service in the home and community.

Love, truth, beauty and harmony are the cornerstones of your world.

You have the innate ability of artistic expression and appreciation.

Seek balance, rhythm and understanding.

7

The 7 is the number of spirituality and mysticism. You are a healer, counselor and minister.

Seek and discover the reality *behind* the appearance; you can be inventive and scientific.

Your destiny is to discover the truth from "within."

The Number	The Description

You are very analytical, comprehensive and contemplative.

Your sense of dignity may make you appear aloof.

You need the finer things in life to experience the joy of living.

Learn to be alone but not lonely; do not insist on partnerships.

Gain understanding and wisdom.

8

The "ORGANIZER"; you have natural executive ability as you are efficient and capable.

You are to improve the lot of mankind through your understanding of human nature and weaknesses.

Watch a tendency to be dictatorial which could lessen your effectiveness and accomplishment.

You should be involved in the business/commercial/financial world.

To understand the laws that govern money and to pass on that understanding to others.

Exercise power with justice and mercy; see that all enjoy freedom of action.

You have an excellent sense of "intuitive" judgment.

9

As the "HUMANITARIAN" you must be objective and have a universal outlook on life.

Try to understand the mysteries of metaphysics and the meaning behind psychic experiences and the occult sciences.

Service in/with humanitarian organizations is emphasized whether it is political/social, spiritual/metaphysical or medical/psychological.

Your greatest success will come in a public environment, with the many rather than the few.

As an idealist, you must guard yourself against moodiness, timidness and vacillation.

Teaching, healing, writing, music and art are all natural arenas for you.

The force and energy of the #9 vibrational pattern make it dynamic and emotional in nature.

11

This is the Master Number of ILLUMINATION which says, "Your light must shine across the land."

Your intuition will show you the way, so have faith in your inner guidance.

You are idealistic and inspirational; you must inspire by your own example, by living your own ideals.

You belong to the public as a Superdiplomat or Peacemaker.

Develop your talents of *invention;* you could excel in TV/Motion Picture/Radio/Literary fields.

Investigate mystical/spiritual principles and put them to their highest use.

You may be an agnostic due to your environment and responses from others while you were growing up.

22

You can become a *MASTER* CARPENTER, MASON or BUILDER.

Your natural arena includes international movements, from commercial to philanthropic to political activities.

The more respect you command, the greater the heights you can reach.

You can become a diplomat, statesman, ambassador, organizer or executive manager.

Success can be yours in real estate, as a financier, as a promoter, or as a Super-athlete or explorer.

Learn to be both inspirational and practical.

Be of service on a large and constructive scale.

6
Goal Power Numbers
Final Opportunities

In the last half of your life, the vibrational patterns of your Goal Power or Final Opportunity Number begin to unfold, providing some of the predominant influences on the remaining experiences of your life. This final Opportunity Number is found by adding the number of your Purpose to the number of your Destiny (see Illustration 6a.). The combination of your birthname and birthdate provides you with the patterns which lead to what is known as the "integration" of your intuition and intellect.

This integration provides you with the understanding of environmental patterns which are in tune with the total development of your life experiences. You can take full advantage of these unfolding patterns simply by preparing yourself for the events and situations indicated by your Goal Power Number.

Your Goal Power Number brings together the aspects of your intuitive perspective (name at birth) and your intellectual perspective (date of birth) to develop for you an additional arena of experiencing. If you can get in tune with these Goal Power Vibrational Patterns by your middle to late 30's, you will find the final half of your life exciting and fulfilled. You can let your life experiences help you gain knowledge, develop your talents, and align you with your patterns of success. Then you can move into the influences of this final opportunity pattern smoothly, rapidly and naturally toward the achievement of your life goals.

The Goal Power or Final Opportunity Number is really saying that if you get your intellectual perspective (how you think about things) together with your intuitive perspective (hunches), and if you develop both of those aspects to their fullest, you will then have an incredibly exciting final half of life.

Real freedom comes during this last half of life, not necessarily in the first half. That's the time to shed past burdens and insecurities and concentrate on experiencing the "finer" goals of your life.

There are too many numerologists who short change the value of our names because they can be changed so easily. But notwithstanding that fact, your name at birth is your identity at birth, whether you like your birthname or not; whether you change your name or not. And it plays a major role in the developing environmental patterns of your life. The language of the numbers of your birthname, in conjunction with your birthdate, establish the framework for a successful and rewarding life. For, as you learn to get in tune with the unfolding patterns of your life experiences, all the creative channels of your being open up: Intuitive, Emotional, Physical and Intellectual.

ILLUSTRATION 6a.

THE INTEGRATION OF INTELLECT AND INTUITION

Finding Your Goal Power Number

Chaldean Alphabet/Number System*

1 2 3 4 5 6 7 8

A B C D E U O F
I K G M H V Z P
J R L T N W
Q S X
Y

Your Goal Power/Final Opportunity Number is found by adding the number of your *Birthdate* (Destiny), your *intellectual* perspective to your *Birthname* number (Purpose), your *intuitive* perspective.

BIRTHDATE NUMBER: September 21, 1938   = $\underline{6}$ (Intellect)
(See Chapter 5)

+

BIRTHNAME NUMBER: WILLIAM PHILLIP MIKE = $\underline{6}$ (Intuition)
(See Chapter 2)

**

GOAL POWER/FINAL OPPORTUNITY NUMBER   = 12 = $\underline{3}$

* The Chaldean/Vedic/Qaballic systems did not assign the #9 to any letter. In the ancient "mystery" schools of knowledge, the #9 was considered the most "sacred" of numbers. Its vibratory force included the attributes of all numbers and, therefore, did not (could not) represent any individual symbol.

** See Chapter 10 for Compound Number meanings.

GOAL POWER OR
FINAL OPPORTUNITY NUMBER
The Sum of Your Birthname and Birthdate

The Number	The Description
1	You will have the opportunity to fill a "Leadership" role, or to be a "Pioneer" of "new" ideas. Your creative originality will be enhanced.

The Number	The Description
	Independence and action can be yours, if you prepare for it.
	Being *over-dominant,* opinionated or "too" set in your views could dampen your success.
2	You could enjoy great success as an Arbiter or Peace-maker or Advisor or Consultant.
	Involve yourself in the arts, such as music, dancing or art.
	You are a gatherer of data; use it.
	Your "bywords" are cooperation and association.
	Don't bend over backwards "too" much in working with others, or you could become a doormat.
3	Self expression is the keynote of this vibration—in speaking, writing or acting.
	Public Speaker, Entertainer, Publisher, or Movie Director are fertile areas for success and fulfillment.
	You are a natural with words, have an excellent imagination and a good sense of humor.
	Avoid scattering yourself and concentrate on a few "select" goals.
4	You can become a "Cosmic Mason" and lay the foundations upon which others can build their dreams.
	You can achieve success in either the scientific or the religious arena.
	You will be able to promote goodwill through sympathy, orderliness and honesty.
	Success and a rewarding outcome will come through hard work, discipline and attention to detail.
5	Yours can be a life of freedom, movement and action, by letting go of the old and learning the untried.

The Number	The Description

The fields of communications, writing, reporting or investigating are natural environments for you.

You can be a salesman, a speculator (whether it is real estate, stocks or gambling) and a travellcr.

Avoid being *too* diversified or reaching out in *too* many directions.

6   Work with an objective or impersonal view of things (detached but not indifferent).

You will find a great deal of success and fulfillment in service to family or community.

You should find satisfaction in your home life and financially in your career.

As a "Cosmic Teacher and Parent," your responsibilities and duties lie in helping and guiding others.

7   Intellectual and spiritual goals will bring you your greatest success.

You could become an "Educator" of great wisdom and understanding.

Great insights can come to you through meditations and contemplation.

You can achieve fulfillment by way of scientific pursuits or inventions or as a metaphysical writer.

Avoid the desire to become an introvert which will limit your experiencing.

8   Opportunities in positions of authority, power and judgment will offer themselves to you.

Supervision, direction and counseling are in the forefront.

Success will require discipline and determination in the exercise of executive and directive abilities.

You can easily achieve recognition and fame in your chosen field.

If the field is financial/commercial, you may be drawn to real estate or banking; if the field is law, your goal can be realized as a judge.

9   This is the vibration of humanitarian and universal pursuits.

Opportunities for fulfillment will come to you more through a "larger" view of things than through a "personal" view.

You can achieve goals of success in the medical, political or philosophical arenas—doctor, nurse, psychiatrist, metaphysician or political office holder.

You can shine as a writer and lecturer on subjects that deal with service to humanity.

11   Many spiritual and religious leaders fall under the "11" vibration.

Limelight, leadership and distinction are signified.

The opportunity for success by way of the "public" platform is indicated—through passing on of inspirational and uplifting ideals.

Since the "11" is electrical in nature, communications fields are open to you—television, radio arena.

Opportunities will also avail themselves to you in high "energy" fields such as aviation, aerospace or electronics including inventions.

22   This is the number of international fame and activity, if a good foundation is established.

You can be the "builder" in the practical or physical world as well as in the world of ideals and metaphysics.

You can succeed as a Statesman, Ambassador or as the Leader of a world organization.

As you work for yourself, *also* work for humanity and your success will be enhanced.

7
Pinnacles
Opportunities, Open Doors

How many times have you felt or "sensed" that major changes were about to occur in your life, but you couldn't define or explain precisely what you meant or were feeling? Many new opportunities seem to come to you unrelated to your current patterns that you are experiencing, yet, the change appears to foreshadow a total shift in career, mental outlook, emotional attitudes and the direction or focus of your life's energies.

Have you ever wondered why and how it happens? So many people between the ages of 25 and 35 seem to question the direction of their lives. "Where am I going?" they keep asking themselves. Oftentimes they will seek counseling to "get life straightened out" when all they really need to have done was to understand the language of their numbers as revealed by their "Pinnacles."

Your first Pinnacle *ends* when you are between the ages of 27 and 36 (see Illustration 7a. to find your Pinnacles). It has a major impact on your life and you may, indeed, feel like your life has shifted into a different gear as it is ending. You can expect another major change of the same sort between the ages of 45 and 55 when you enter what is known as your "Final Pinnacle." Both are exciting opportunities to move closer to mastering your blueprint and have an enormous impact on your life experiences.

ILLUSTRATION 7a

OPPORTUNITIES, OPEN DOORS

Finding the Numbers of Your Pinnacles

BIRTHDATE: September 21, 1938   = <u>6</u> (Destiny)

FIRST PINNACLE: *Add* the number of your birth *month* to the number of your *day* at birth.

September 21, 1938

$$9 \; + \; 3 \quad = \; 12 \; = \; \underline{3}$$

The length of this pinnacle is found by *subtracting* your birthdate number (Destiny) from the #36; i.e., 36 − 6 = *30 years* duration. This pinnacle begins at birth—until 1968.

SECOND PINNACLE: *Add* the number of your *day* of birth to the number of your birth *year*.

September 21, 1938

$$3 + 3 \; = \; \underline{6}$$

The length of this pinnacle is *9 years* to 1977.

THIRD PINNACLE: *Add* the number of the *First* Pinnacle to the number of the *Second* Pinnacle.

$$3 \; + \; 6 \; = \; \underline{9}$$

The length of this pinnacle is 9 years to 1986.

FOURTH (final) PINNACLE: *Add* the number of your birth *month* to the number of your birth *year*.

September 21, 1938

$$9 \qquad + \qquad 3 \; = \; 12 \; = \; \underline{3}$$

This pinnacle goes from 1986 onward.

PINNACLES
Opportunities, Open Doors

The Number	The Description
1	Beginning of a 9-year cycle will bring new projects, change and action.

The Number	The Description

You will have a chance to individualize and be independent.

You may find yourself in a leadership role.

Your creativity and originality will be in the forefront.

Stand on your own two feet and rely on your own abilities for success.

Be aware of obstinancy or domineering attitude.

2

You will have an opportunity for accumulation through cooperation.

Cultivate diplomacy, harmony and patience.

This is a better period for partnerships and associations than for individual endeavors.

Pay attention to detail.

Don't be insensitive to others; *share.*

3

Develop your creative/artistic ability; imagination and feelings will be on top; use them.

You may have opportunities for writing, speaking, interior designing and stage/movie entertainment.

Put forth effort to channel your creative talent for your greatest success; don't scatter yourself.

4

This is a period for building and preparation for the future.

Hard work will be required as well as constant service and effort; a slow but sure period.

Maintain order; be systematic; put facts and ideas in order.

Take time to put your ideas into practical form.

Inner Response—discard old; make ready for expansion.

5

This is a period of freedom, movement and change.

The Number	The Description

Let go of old and accept new.

You may experience restlessness and uncertainty.

Bywords are versatility, activity, travel, new experiences, new friends.

Advertising, selling, promotional activities are enhanced.

Curb tendency to act impulsively.

 6

Home duties and responsibilities are emphasized.

Cultivate love and willing service.

Money can be made through much work and settling down.

Happiness results from giving and helping others as well as your own family (not a pinnacle for personal interests only).

Pinnacle of marriage—if you do, it will be a good one.

7

Interest should be in spiritual progress, not material.

Study metaphysics, philosophy and knowledge in general.

Inner response should be one of poise, self examination and waiting.

You may feel aloof, depressed, moody and restricted; *Don't* withdraw or retreat.

Be honest, patient and understanding, or difficulty may result in personal relationships or partnerships.

8

This is an excellent period for financial/material gain, but demands courage, strength, ambition and constant effort.

You can obtain a position of authority and fame by exercising good judgment.

Do not rely on luck; but do rely on your ability to make sound judgments.

The Number	The Description
	Laziness or lack of ambition will cause delays and struggle.
9	Learn to love and give without expecting anything in return; a highly charged and emotional period which could be difficult.
	Learn to be impersonal and universal, not aiming for personal relationships and it will be rewarding.
	Develop compassion, tolerance and service to others.
	Inner Response—love, sympathy and selflessness.
11	This is a pinnacle of spiritual expansion, illumination and fame.
	Cultivate inventiveness.
	You may experience nervousness and tension, since this is an "electrical period."
	Much will be expected of you and your talents.
	You will have the opportunity to be in the limelight and public arena.
22	International affairs and wordly activities should be promoted.
	This is a period for the expansion of consciousness.
	You will have an opportunity to flourish both materially and idealistically.
	In order to bring success to fruition, you must think BIG and for the benefit of the world.

8
Meeting Your Challenges
Strengthening Your Abilities

"Ask, and it will be given you; seek, and you will find; knock and it will be opened to you." Matthew 7:7

Challenges are closed doors which will open for you and all you have to do is knock. They are situations, events, circumstances, and/or people operating in your environment which can help you strengthen those abilities which will prepare you for the onset of greater opportunities.

You have a *Main Challenge*, whose influences will be felt throughout your life. You also have three *Sub-Challenge* cycles. The first one influences your life until you are between the ages of 25 and 35. Then a "change" usually occurs in the second sub-challenge which lasts 27 years. The third and final sub-challenge affects the last part of your life.

The impact of these cycle changes is magnified because of their concurrent shift with those of the First Pinnacle and the Final Pinnacle discussed in Chapter 7.

Meeting your challenges can strengthen your chances for success and *open doors* to additional experiencing and participating in your life.

ILLUSTRATION 8a

STRENGTHEN YOUR ABILITIES

Finding the Numbers of Your Challenges

BIRTHDATE: September 21, 1938

FIRST SUB-CHALLENGE: *Subtract* the number of your *day* of birth from the number of your birth *month*.

September 21, 1938

$$9 - 3 = \underline{6}$$

(*ignore* any minus — sign in the answer)

The length of this Sub-Challenge is the same as the First Pinnacle, *30 years* to 1968.

SECOND SUB-CHALLENGE: *Subtract* the number of your birth *year* from the number of your *day* of birth.

September 21, 1938

$$3 - 3 = \underline{0}$$

This Sub-Challenge is *27 years* long, to 1995.

MAIN CHALLENGE: *Subtract* the number of the *Second* Sub-challenge from the number of the *First* Sub-Challenge.

$$6 - 0 = \underline{6}$$

The Main Challenge is with you always.

THIRD (final) SUB-CHALLENGE: *Subtract* the number of your birth *year* from the number of your birth *month*.

September 21, 1938

$$9 - 3 = \underline{6}$$

This Sub-Challenge is *27 years* long.

CHALLENGES
Abilities to be Strengthened

The Number	The Description
1	Develop willpower, strength of courage and character. You could be (have been) put down by relatives/friends (or held back).

The Number	The Description

Keep from vacillating to please others and accomplish nothing.

For success, many interferences must be overcome.

Work to remove chips of resentment and belligerence.

Develop and apply creative ideas; command the respect of others.

Make sure you are right, then go straight ahead, firmly.

2

Cultivate a broad viewpoint; don't refer everything to yourself, for you are sensitive and will find it hard to forgive and forget.

Develop self-confidence; don't be a doormat or afraid—BE YOURSELF.

Don't get caught up in "little things" that will drag you down.

Don't be nice or hold back truth just to make an impression.

Don't copy; use your own talents.

Your psychic power is inherent so don't sell it—USE it!

3

You must make social contacts, enjoy people and socialize.

You must be a "butterfly" not a mouse.

GO PUBLIC: work for and become involved in public affairs.

Avoid scattering your talents, energy or effort.

You must cultivate your artistic abilities—writing, speaking, art, dancing, music and any creative expression—then many doors will be opened for you.

4

Pay *attention* not to be opinionated and stubborn; it could hold back your success.

Discipline yourself to be orderly, systematic and punctual.

You may dislike routine jobs, tend to put off things or

The Number	The Description
	worry *needlessly;* all of these are traps which will hold you back.
	You have a tendency to force things; DON'T. You should just let things happen and unfold naturally.
5	DO NOT seek freedom in order to escape responsibilities.
	A heightened interest in sex and the senses may make you impulsive.
	You want freedom at any price.
	Learn the lesson of discard—what to let go and when to let it go.
	Do not change simply for the sake of change.
	The right use of your desire for freedom can make you successful at promotion, advertising, travel or publicity.
6	You are overly idealistic about what is wrong and right.
	You may be opinionated and righteous.
	Must learn to respect, not just tolerate, the views of others for true companionship and love.
	Don't expect or try to make everyone adjust or conform to "your" rules or way of thinking; you will be resented; adjust to the fact that everyone is entitled to their own point of view.
7	You are rebellious against prevailing conditions; you must alter or better those conditions.
	Beware of false pride, aloofness and reserve which keep your real feelings buried.
	Develop keen analysis and technical skills.
	Do not dwell on what you think are your limitations.
	Do not stay at war with yourself.
	Develop faith in your own self-worth and soul.
8	Opportunities for recognition and success are excellent, *IF* your motives are straight forward and aboveboard.

The Number	The Description
	You have a delusionary sense of values in that you are afraid of loss and limitation, and as a result you experience lack and limitation.

This is known as the "Balance of Power" challenge; you must see both the material side and the spiritual side of power and money and bring them into balance

You believe that personal freedom is based on material possessions.

0   The "zero" challenge is known as the challenge of "CHOICE"; you have reached a point in your development where you may "choose" for yourself and cannot rely on others choosing for you.

You must make your own decisions in life and *know* where your pitfalls lie.

You have the knowledge and talents of all the numbers.

You know which way to turn, but you must know that you *know*, and then—*CHOOSE!*

9

Tuning In to
What's Coming Up

Personal Years and Months

Personal Years

The Personal Year influences, which are derived from the birthdate, are also aspects of your blueprint. When you enter a particular year, you find that year unfolding within a certain pattern. The vibrations are set up to develop the *potential* for events and situations, and for associations that "fit" a general descriptive pattern within a particular environment. By knowing the potential experiences which are reflected in the vibrational patterns of your personal years you can use your resources to your greatest advantage.

The numbers of the Personal Year give you a "mini" blueprint of your potential experiences. You can take advantage of all the things within it, and move all of the activities you choose in the direction you want to take them.

If you are told of a highway to take to your destination which would help you to avoid obstacles and delay, and it would have the scenic route, but you ignored the advice, and lost your way, you could only blame yourself. It is not the fault of the map or the directions given. It's the decision not to pay attention to information that is valid and helpful. Understanding the language of your personal years can help you plan your trip.

To find the "number" of your Personal Year, first take the number of the month of your birthday and add it to the number of the day of your birthday. (See Illustration 9a.). Then add it to the number of the current

UNIVERSAL Year. For instance, if your birthday is September 21, the number of the month is "9." The number of the day, 21, is 2 plus 1 equals "3." Choose the Universal Year which is the closest to the birthday. September 21, *1979* is *closest* to the Universal Year 1980. The "number" of 1980 is 1 plus 9 plus 8 which equals 18, and 1 plus 8 equal "9." Add the number 9 of the month to the number 3 of the day to the number 9 of the year. This equals 21. The "number" of the Personal Year then equals "3" (2 plus 1).

Your Personal Year *always* begins on your birthday, and is defined by the vibrational pattern of the "number" of your Personal Year. If your birthday falls in the last half of the calendar year (July 1 through December 31), the date of the following year will determine the number of the Universal Year to be used in deriving your Personal Year. This is because the vibrational pattern of the following year "pulls" you forward under its influence. That vibration becomes a "magnet" which draws you toward it. It is also indicative of our natural state being that of "flowing" with our experiences rather than being pushed into anything.

The important thing to know about your Personal Year Vibrational Patterns is that the more you prepare to take advantage of them, the greater the satisfaction and success and the easier the action is accomplished.

In a number 1 year, you create the idea and plan to put it into action. You begin things—such as a new position at work, a new job, a new book, a new association. In a number 2 year you build on the idea; you develop partnerships; you work in cooperation with others. In a number 3 Personal Year you experience a "cycle" of fruition; you express the idea; you express yourself—in writing, in lecturing, in singing, etc. In a number 4 year you give form to the idea; you go about your business by detailing plans for a foundation or basis from which you can expand activity; you consolidate; you keep your nose to the grind and take advantage of the business of hard work so that you can prepare for a very big year of action in your number 5 Personal Year. The number 5 year is one of action, change, movement, variety and expansion. Promote the idea; advertise yourself and your abilities. You will be able to handle many projects at the same time (although not simultaneously).

When you don't flow with the patterns of your personal years, you may be in tune to a prior year when the new year is already upon you. You are not ready to take full advantage of the new and end up still doing "old" things in the new environment, wondering why things seem to be out of sync.

From the action of the "5" year, you move into a "6" year which is a year of adjustment, balance, harmony. You relax and enjoy the arts; you find material reward which you share with others; you can take advantage of additional learning; educational projects flourish. Bring things into focus by taking advantage of the calming effect of the number 6. From the calm outward enjoyment of the number 6 year, you move under the influence of the vibrational pattern of the number 7. It is a year of introspection, self-evaluation, self-analysis; you can find the "peace that passes all understanding." Bring things together on an inner level, knowing that your table is already prepared before you and nothing can stop you from finding complete fulfillment in your upcoming experiences. You don't have to push for things to happen; just let them happen. Meditate on your own inner power and what it can accomplish for you. Tie up loose ends. Your rest and meditation will build your reservoir of energy which you will put to great use in your number 8 Personal Year. In the number 8 Personal Year, you can direct the movement of the action. You can sign business contracts with confidence (as long as you "guided" the writing of it). It is a business/finance/commercial activity year. If you prepare for it, it can be very materially rewarding. Your "hunches" (intuition) will be accurate and your judgment will be excellent.

The language of numbers permits you to "see" what's coming up and how to prepare for it. Each Personal Year's Vibrational Pattern being a "mini" blueprint within your major blueprint, is available to you anytime you want to see it—a year from now or ten years from now.

The number 9 year is a very exciting and highly emotional year, in the sense that your emotions will be so finely tuned and charged that you may end up taking things too personally when you shouldn't. You will be emotionally sensitive in the number 9 year which is such an energetic, forceful and highly charged year that you become highly charged. It is a year in which the more objective you are and the more universal your outlook, the more you will find satisfaction. However, you can find great excitement through your emotional involvement, if you don't exhaust yourself. If you have never truly experienced your emotions, the number 9 year can give you the widest possible set of choices for experiencing and the greatest opportunity to feel through the entire range of emotions that you have.

Personal Months

The Personal *Month* is derived simply by taking the number of your Personal Year and adding it to the number of the *Universal* Month. (See Illustration 9b.). For instance, your Personal Month Vibration Pattern for the month of May is found by adding the number of your Personal Year to the number of May (Universal Month) which is number 5.

The month's universal pattern generates an "umbrella" effect relative to your personal month patterns; i.e., you function within your vibrations, but with the overtone of the universal vibrations. The same governing effect is operating on your personal years, but with the reference to the Universal Year Vibrational Pattern.

The nature of universal vibrational patterns are such that we really have no control over them. This is especially true in regard to shaping or supplying the variations of the environmental patterns, the potential events, and the indicated situations. However, we do determine which events we want to participate in, thereby shaping *our* patterns and as such impinging on, interfering with, or adding to the direction in which these universal vibrational patterns seem to be moving.

The greater your participation in your *experiences,* the greater your influence on the events unfolding. I *didn't say* the greater the participation in *worldly* events, the greater your influence. You cannot influence universal events, only your own. Your only control over universal vibrations is the fact that you chose to experience a certain set of events or environmental patterns represented by those universal vibrations. I speak of it because of the fact that you find your Personal Year by taking the Universal Year Number and *personalizing* it by adding your personal month and day of birth to it, thereby drawing or "using" the universal vibrations in developing your personalized set of events.

The meanings of the monthly vibrational patterns must be understood relative to the nature of the "span of time" available. The monthly time period "moves" very quickly, so that you must take advantage of the aspects you wish to use and take part in the "optimum" events, by preparing for them before they occur, or at least planning for them. You will begin to feel the vibrational influence of the next month as you move into the last week of the current month. And, although the vibrational pattern of your current personal month still governs, you will react to some of the influence of the following month's personal vibrations.

When we work with the language of the vibrational patterns of our Personal Years and Months we are simply getting in tune with the action of the coming periods of experiences (not periods of time, but periods of action, participation, and experiencing).

In using the information that's available to you through the language of your numbers, you do not nor should not get caught in the trap of living your life by your numbers, no more than one should live their lives by their stars or by the words of their teachers, or counselors, or any other framework of concepts, ideas or dogmas. However, you can take advantage of the unfolding events to your benefit by familiarizing yourself with the general pattern of your personal numbers. Then you allow yourself to be flexible in taking part in the unfolding experiences that present themselves to you. For events or happenings which are special or of great importance, to you, you can get more "specific" in the information you wish to use from the personal vibrations of your numbers. You will find that the event or happening will occur with greater ease and result in greater satisfaction to you when you use the language of your numbers.

ILLUSTRATION 9a

YEARLY CYCLES

Finding the Numbers of Your Personal Years

A Personal Year number is found by adding the number of your *birth month* to the number of your *day of birth,* then adding that sum to the number of the *calendar year* (closest to your birthday) in which you are interested. Calendar years are known as UNIVERSAL YEARS.

UNIVERSAL YEAR NUMBERS

1972 = 1	1982 = 2	1992 = 3
1973 = 2	1983 = 3	1993 = 4 (22)
1974 = 3	1984 = 4 (22)	1994 = 5
1975 = 4 (22)	1985 = 5	1995 = 6
1976 = 5	1986 = 6	1996 = 7
1977 = 6	1987 = 7	1997 = 8
1978 = 7	1988 = 8	1998 = 9
1979 = 8	1989 = 9	1999 = 1
1980 = 9	1990 = 1	2000 = 2
1981 = 1	1991 = 2	2001 = 3

EXAMPLE: Birthday = May 15 ;   Find the Personal Year Number for 1980 for this birthday.

May 15, 1980

5 + 6 + 9 (See table above) = 20

Personal Year Number = 2 + 0 = <u>2</u>

For the birth month and day which fall on or after July 1 of the year, use the *following* Universal Year number in the calculation.

YEARLY CYCLES
The Numbers of Your Personal Years

The Number	The Description
1	This ushers in a new nine year cycle; welcome change and novelty.

The Number	The Description
	This is a good year to make plans and put them into action.
	If you wish to start something new, the number "1" year is an excellent time to begin.
	When you meet new associates, lasting friendships should develop.
	You must stand on your own two feet and be individual in your action.
	Your creative and inventive powers are at their peak.
	It is a time of work, organization and clear thinking.
2	A receptive/cooperative attitude brings you your greatest success.
	Form a union, choose collaborators, business associates or lifemate.
	Important matters on an emotional plane may be exaggerated.
	Develop tact and diplomacy.
	This is a cycle for building—a new home, career or mansion for your soul.
	Don't launch any new major projects; you may feel weighed down by details.
	If you work with and act on your own intuition, psychic illuminations, inspiration and limelight can be yours.
3	The number "3" is known as the cycle of fruition or success; it can be a "lucky" year if your efforts and money are not scattered and your energies are concentrated on *priority* goals.
	You should find popularity with friends, large groups and in the public.
	For you, "self expression" is the keynote in both the spoken and written word; take care and diligence in what you say, write and *sign*; be sure you read the fine print and understand what you are reading or hearing.

The Number	The Description

This can be a good selling period; market whatever you put into words.

4
The "4" year is a building year in the sense of detailing out plans and developing a good framework for future action.

Make proper "connections", put your "nose to the grind" and *save.*

Don't let the feeling of restriction keep you from growing; consolidate and retrench, for soon you will be very active.

Although expansion will be slow, it will be positive.

This is a good cycle for firm friendships, balance in family relationships as well as for engagement or marriage.

5
Freedom of action should be emphasized; it should bring change, travel, motion and expansion.

The number "5" is a "cycle" of *words*—writing, lecturing, singing, radio, television, communications industries (public relations, advertising, etc.).

You will find new people, new places, new situations continually.

It is a time to get out of a rut or lose beautiful experiences.

Don't scatter yourself; let each new experience be of use to you in your process of learning and growing.

6
This brings to you a cycle of education and learning, balance and adjustment.

As a year of responsibility (domestic), you will be able to create beauty and harmony in your environment.

Don't plan to be "too" personal in your desires—you will be needed in many directions.

Finish all you undertake; be thorough and conscientious.

The Number	The Description

This period should see you free of occupational and major financial problems.

7
The "peace that passeth understanding" can be yours this year.

Pursue spiritual, mental, intellectual activities, including meditation and philosophy.

Use your intuitive powers; seek spiritual enlightenment.

This will be a slow period; you could experience delays. It will pass.

You may feel physical energy at a low ebb; take care not to overdue things.

This is a period of mental housecleaning, reflection and perfection.

The desire to withdraw and the feeling of aloneness may come over you, which also will pass, but use the time for *introspection* and get acquainted with your self.

Do not "brood" over the past—simply look at it and **put it where it belongs; this is a period of waiting; await developments, don't force them; let things come to you.**

8
This is a period when you can avail yourself of energy, force, power, discipline and good judgment.

Devote this year to planning, organization and action.

Opportunities for advancement and success in business and financial affairs will present themselves to you.

This is also a cycle of philanthropy; volunteer your time and services to a worthwhile organization or cause for much satisfaction.

You will find that greater freedom will be yours this year than you have had for quite a long time.

9
The number "9" year is known as the year of ending and the year of beginning; you are closing out a nine year cycle to begin.

The Number	The Description
	It will be a year of energy, force and change; it is a time to cast off old attitudes and non-constructive habits.
	You must be willing to let go of old things that are no longer valid for you, if you want to be ready for your number "1" year.
	Try to look at things impersonally or objectively (but not with indifference).
	You are getting ready for the new and cannot be burdened by the old.
	You may experience the feeling of indecision during the year; this is due to the fact that many decisions will have to be made.
11	This is a "Master Year" and can be filled with inspiration and psychic illumination.
	If you permit yourself to "go with" your intuition and act on your "hunches", it can be a year of limelight and fame.
	Our inner ideals illumine everything we do; your greatest success will come by following your "inner" principles.
	This will be a year of religious and metaphysical matters; you could very well be involved in a great deal of activity in these areas.
22	This vibration is the number "4" elevated; it is known as the year of "universal appeal".
	You will find great rewards through working in the name of humanity and the world.
	You should find yourself with deep involvement in humanitarian organizations and foundations.
	The "sky is the limit" should be your theme.
	This is a year when your dreams can be "actualized" and brought into form.

ILLUSTRATION 9b

MONTHLY CYCLE

Finding the Numbers of Your Personal Months

A Personal Month number is found by adding the *number of your Personal Year* to the *calendar month* in which you are interested. Calendar month numbers are known as UNIVERSAL MONTH numbers.

UNIVERSAL MONTH NUMBERS

January	= 1	July	=	7
February	= 2	August	=	8
March	= 3	September	=	9
April	= 4	October	=	1
May	= 5	November	=	2
June	= 6	December	=	3

EXAMPLE: Birthday = September 21, 1979

Find the Personal Month number for the month of March 1980. In this case, 1980 is "closest" to this birthday, and therefore, is the Universal Year number to be used.

Personal Year number = September 21, 1980 = 3

9 + 3 + 9 = 21 = 3

Personal Month number = 3 (Personal year) +

3 (Universal Month) = 6

MONTHLY CYCLES
The Numbers of Your Personal Months

The Number	The Description
1	This is a favorable period for associations and/or work with men.
	This is a beneficial time for expressing your ambitions.
	Your ability to make progress is enhanced.
	New beginnings, new projects, new associates are emphasized.

The Number	The Description

This cycle could be signified by you becoming the main figure in an organization; if you take the first step.

2   This cycle is keynoted by cooperation, coordination, highlighted by partnership and receptivity.

Associations and/or work with women is emphasized.

This is a time for practicality as well as "follow through" effort.

Your creative imagination is active—USE it!

3   This should be a period when you have a happy, positive outlook.

Social popularity is emphasized as well as many dealings with clubs and organizations.

If your talents and energy are not scattered, it could be a very successful time for you.

Watch your desire to spend money—be wise!

4   You are in a "building cycle" and should sacrifice now for future benefits.

This cycle is restrictive in nature, in the sense of needing to pay attention to detail; it is one of "*busy*ness."

Discipline yourself and work with determination.

Success will follow you more easily if you develop and express tolerance, mercy and sympathy.

5   This is a period of change, travel and movement.

You should experience many and varied situations, people and events; this includes associations and acquaintances.

Religious and spiritual work is signified (evangelistic in nature).

This is an excellent time for speaking, writing and salesmanship, including promoting your own ideas.

Beware of haste or speed in your decisions.

The Number	The Description

6 The "6" cycle symbolizes the law of balance and responsibility.

You should earn good money, but may be required to share it with many.

This is a good period for study projects and gaining knowledge.

Married life and romance are highlighted.

You will find great enjoyment in things involved in rhythm, beauty, culture and fine arts.

7 This is a good period for intellectual pursuits (quiet pleasures of the mind).

Pursue studies of a mystical nature.

This cycle is one in which you can put ideas into form.

Be punctual; don't let delays cause disappointment.

You can carry out plans in which personal contact is unnecessary.

Be aware of a tendency to feel alone and lonely (it is a good period to contact your "center," but not to withdraw from the action).

8 Force, energy and power are at your command during this cycle.

You should now be able to avail yourself of what is at hand.

Take the reins of your action and participation and set your own direction.

NOTE: Power has been entrusted to you—use discretion.

9 This is a very good period to eliminate negative influences.

This cycle is signified by balance, growth and gain.

Cast off old (no longer valid) modes, ways and attitudes, and cheerfully make way for the new.

The Number	The Description

The best use of this vibration comes from service to others—humanitarian associations.

11 This "Master Number" vibration should find your intuition humming. Visions, revelations and psychic illumination are emphasized. This cycle is keynoted by metaphysics, philosophy and religion. You may be given the opportunity for "limelight" events. This period is good for promoting and launching an invention.

22 Put the combination of material and spiritual to work.

This "Master Vibration" is good for laying the foundations for humanitarian activities.

International and worldly affairs are emphasized during this cycle.

Under the influence of the "22," you can make your dreams a reality.

10
Reading Between the Lines
The Meaning of Compound Numbers

One of the most exciting aspects of Numerology is the interpretation of Compound Numbers. In the study of the language of numbers (Numerolinguistics), Compound Numbers permit one to "read between the lines." The numbers that I will cover will range from the 10 through the 54. In the text of this chapter I will discuss certain specific numbers, including the 11, 13, 18, 19, 22, 23 and some of the Compound Numbers which are generally considered "negative" in nature.

To get the full benefit of the meaning of Compound Numbers in interpreting the language of anyone's numbers, you must look at the interacting influences of all of the numbers "within" the Compound Number. This process permits you to see "why" some of the Compound Numbers have been misunderstood and misinterpreted as negative.

The first number of the Compound Number is the "dominant" influence, while the second number supports, accents, or creates an underlying environment pattern in which the "first" number operates and functions. At the center of each Compound Number is its "root," derived by adding the individual numbers of the Compound Number together until you have a single digit. The vibrational patterns of this "root" number set the *"tone"* for the Compound Number's environmental impact.

Certain of the Compound Numbers have "compound" numbers within them as well as the root number. Examples of these numbers are

#29 = 11 = 2 (11 is a Compound Number within a Compound Number and the #2 is the root number), #37 = 10 = 1, #39 = 12 = 3, and the #49 = 13 = 4. The vibrational patterns of the Compound Numbers within the Compound Number also have an influence on the unfolding environment of the original number.

Most numerologists doom certain Compound Numbers to some tragic and dreaded future. When anyone comes in contact with those numbers, all that they can think of is the picture of "negativity" which has been painted. In reality, it is not the number which causes the negativity, nor can a number bring misfortune with it. Negativity and misfortune are the results of misinterpretation, miscalculation and misunderstanding.

For instance, in most if not all reference materials, the #16 is considered a very negative number, portending danger and hardship. In studying the language of numbers, you will find that this is a distortion of the truth of such numbers. With a vibrational pattern such as the #16 has, you have three things occurring which cause people to misinterpret or distort what is happening within the vibrational influence of the 16. You have the #1 present, the #6, the #7 which is the #16 root. The #1 is the individual, the leader, the pioneer. The #6 is the number of dedication to family and service to the community as well as harmony and balance. This results in an initial seeming conflict, between the leadership, upfront, stage center, vibrations of the #1, and the #6 which says service to family and community—where family and community (not the individual) is number one. Now tie that in with the vibratory influence of the root #7. The #7 includes patterns which reflect the vibrational aspects of the "loner," the meditative, introspective and analytical approach to things.

You also have the law of preservation influencing the environment. The law of preservation rules the #16. The #7 seeks to preserve the "truth." The #6 is the number of the "family," preserving the family unit. The #1 is the vibration which emphasizes the preservation of the "ego," or the individuality. Since preservation and survival are part and parcel of the #16 vibration, this brings with it, the need for and the use of caution and care in doing things (taking care to preserve).

You get an interplay of action between all of the patterns of each number within the Compound Number. When something happens in the environment which seems to "fit" the #16 and at the same time the #16 is showing on the door to an office, the conclusion of the "traditional numerologists" is that the #16 is causing the problem. The real cause of the problem is the failure of those within the environment to understand the nature of the unfolding patterns and events.

Traditionalists continue to say that you should look out for a number such as the #16, because it is negative in its influence. Or they tell you to avoid any number whose vibrational patterns are difficult to interpret. What should be said instead is that when you walk into an environment where the vibrational patterns may cause you uncertainty or discomfort, allow yourself to be aware of the nature of the vibrations which surround you. In that way you will be able to experience your surroundings without misunderstanding or discomfort.

The analysis and evaluation of Compound Numbers which follows has never been undertaken in the detail and scope presented here. I have done it this way to allow for a greater understanding of Compound Numbers. In most existing published information on Compound Numbers, the reader is told "what" a certain number means, but never told why the Compound Number means what it does.

In looking at the meaning and interpretation of Compound Numbers, the zero (0) plays an interesting part. For instance, it means either potential or choice. In relation to one's challenges (closed doors to be opened), it is known as the "Challenge of Choice." In combination with another number, it is a number of potential. The zero (0) gives to the root number what is known as an open endedness and provides an added dimension to the patterns of the single digit root vibration. In other words, it increases its potential.

For instance, in the case of the #10, the zero "increases the potential" of the #1 which is the number of individuality, leadership, pioneering endeavors, thereby enhancing the success of such events operating in the environment of the #10 vibrational patterns. The zero magnifies the abilities and enhances the "honor and prestige" of the root number, while providing a successs orientation whether for seeming "good" or seeming "evil" endeavors.

Numbers are neutral. They are neither good or evil, right or wrong, positive or negative. Whatever you are involved in will move toward success as long as you are in tune and flow with the environmental patterns which are unfolding. If they flow from a Compound Number with a "zero," your chances for success will be increased.

The number 10 is a high vitality number, not only by virtue of the #1 vibrations, but also by virtue of the fact that the #10 starts the cycle of the Compound Numbers. It is the first step or pattern which leads into the process of interpreting the language of the Compound Numbers. The #10 is the symbol (metaphysically) of the return to "wholeness"—having gone the full circle of experiences from the #1 through the #9 and returning to the #1 by way of the #10, which is the #1 raised up in potential. When one learns the "Ten Commandments," they have achieved the "universality" of the #10 (metaphysically). The #10's significance can be seen in the Ten Commandments and the Ten Patriarchs of Israel. In the Old Testament when God spoke to Lot, He said, "If there be ten in the city (Sodom & Gomorrah) who are not sinners, then it would be saved." In the launching of our spacecraft (new beginnings), the countdown starts at 10, 9, 8 . . . zero is the point of liftoff.

The next number is the 11 which I've spoken of before. It is a Master number and has much symbology around it. The #11 represents equilibrium between two extremes. If you have ever seen Greek temples, you become aware of the two upright columns of marble which hold up the roof over the entrance that leads into the temple. It is a number of idealism combined with aspiration, making it a very "charismatic" vibration.

The root number of the 11 is the #2. The #11 is the #2 vibratory force magnified, enhancing the attributes of the #2. Sensitivity is increased; creative imagination is increased; the present ability of "diplomacy" (being able to see both sides) is increased. The two "1's" (double emphasis) enhance creative originality—the #1 being the number of originality and creation. It is a "limelight" number because of a charismatic presence, intensified imagination and creative originality, along with the leadership emphasis of the #1's. The #11 in connection with a "public" event is a very favorable influence.

The #11 is the number of the psychic, the visionary and the dreamer. Intense emotions, dramatic flair and much nervous energy are keyed around the 11. The #11 vibrational pattern is one in which your "intuition" will operate at a very high level.

The #12 has as its root number the 3, which is the number of self expression, of intuition and of integration (the trinity: body, mind and soul). The #3 is a number of ambition, social contact and public endeavor (as a speaker or entertainer). Since it is ambitious, in the sense of being goal oriented (which, in our society, equals the pursuit of money), the #3 is also a number of money.

The #12 has within its patterns, the #1, which being *first* in order, dominates, and brings with it the aspects of leadership, individuality and unity. The #12 has a secondary influence, the vibrational patterns of the #2, which brings with it cooperation, partnership, sensitivity and creative imagination. These two aspects are two numbers which do well when brought together. The number of individuality is combined with the number of cooperation.

The #12's significance is seen in the 12 months of the year, the 12 disciples of Christ, the 12 signs of the Zodiac, the 12 Tribes of Israel, the 12 powers (metaphysical) or faculties of mankind, the 12 hours in the morning and the 12 hours in the afternoon.

Compound Numbers are important in the sense that they reveal additional (between the lines) information about the environment, ensuing events or developing situations which have been identified by the single digit "root" vibrational pattern. A Compound Number also brings with it the identity of certain talents which are latent in its unfolding patterns.

For instance, the number 21 has the root #3, just like the #12. The #21 is the most favorable of the "threes" because the #2 dominates instead of the #1. Cooperation, partnership, receptivity, sensitivity and imagination dominate. This sensitivity and imagination is operating in an environment of individuality, innovation and leadership—which brings new ideas, new beginnings, and new associations. The #21 governs public activities, social events, publishing, entertainment and dramatic endeavors. Anyone who might be involved in theatre arts, singing, dancing or speaking will find the #21 a very favorable pattern within which to perform.

A number which has been considered as *THE* most unlucky number in all of history is, of course, the #13. It is also the most abused of all the numbers. The truth of the matter is that the #13 is not at all an unfortunate number, or questionable in connection with unfolding events surrounding a person.

The misconception is based on the fact that the #13 is a very, very *powerful number* with a very strong and aggressive vibratory force. It is the combination of two of the most "masculine" of the numbers, both directive, active, outward moving and dynamic in nature, the #1 and the #3. The #1 is the number of individuality, leadership, and the pioneering spirit of "blazing new trails." The #3 is the number of ambition, self expression, drive and public endeavors. You have two strong vibrational patterns working in combination with each other—which magnifies and emphasizes their natural attributes and forces.

Whenever anyone walks into an environment which is dominated by the vibratory force of the #13, the vibratory influences are so strong that the environment sometimes becomes too uncomfortable to flow with and as a result "accidents" occur, mistakes are made, or "luck" goes sour. And so naturally, the #13 has been blamed for causing bad luck.

However, BAD LUCK is not caused by the #13. In fact, the #13 is a very good number to have "on one's side," because it brings with it favorable vibrational patterns that can help one achieve success in active endeavors. In addition, the #13 has as its root the number 4, which is the number of the carpenter, of earth, of discipline, of practicality and of dependability. The root vibration of the #4 gives some stability to the #13 by virtue of the "foundation" which the #4 builds as a base to operate from.

If there is any negativity at all about the #13, it would be that creativity may be somewhat hampered or limited, because the #4 is a very structured number and places a "framework" or "box" around the creative potential of the #1 and the #3. Therefore a person *may* feel that their creativity is restricted and limited when they operate within the environment of the #13. But, that does not have to be so.

The significance of the #13 can be seen in the "lost" tribe of Israel which was the 13th tribe. The most significant and outstanding meaning of the #13 is the fact that this nation was established upon the foundation (#4) of 13 original colonies and the 13 stars and stripes of the first flag. America also represents the individual (#1) and self-expression (#3). For America and its people, the #13 was indeed a very "lucky" number.

The #16 which has been discussed earlier, is a very favorable number for things intellectual. It favors an intellectual, mystical or scientific atmosphere and any endeavor which is involved in the search for the truth of reality and existence. It is a good vibrational pattern for educators.

The number 17 is the "best" of the #8 root vibrations. It is made up of the #1 which is creativity, originality and individuality, and the #7 which has the intellectual, scientific and mystical vibrational patterns. As a result, the #17 *demands* "proof" of the validity of things. The #17 person must be shown the proof of the "pudding" (which is in the taste) before they will buy anything. It has behind it the root #8, which is the business, finance and commercial number.

It is particularly successful for endeavors in banking, executives in a corporation, or individuals heading their own businesses.

It is a number of vitality through the courage of the #1 and the power of the #8. It is a comfortable vibrational pattern to work or play in because it brings together the intuition of the #8, the intellectual attributes of the number 7, and the emotional drive of the #1. The root #8 (feminine in nature) brings a great deal of balance to the directness of the 1 and 7 which are masculine and active.

The root of the #18 is the #9 which represents completion, healing, metaphysics, force and energy. It is universal in nature. The #18 combines the independence and leadership of the #1 with the power and judgment of the #8, giving it a very powerful vibrational influence. It is known as the number of great leaders. Great leaders will function very well within an eighteen vibrational pattern or with a #18 influence, particularly if it has anything to do with social, political, or spiritual/metaphysical change or upheaval.

Things spiritual come under the influence of the #18 from the #9 which is the number of healing and metaphysics and from the #8 which is the number of intuition. The number 18 was the number of Jesus Christ. The name Jesus vibrates to the #9 and the name Christ vibrates to the #9.

Therefore, Jesus Christ's mission was the #9 (the #18's root). The number 9 mission is that of the Humanitarian, Metaphysician and Healer. Jesus Christ was the forerunner of the greatest spiritual upheaval in the history of man.

The number 19 is considered the most favorable of all the numbers. The #19 is the individual (#1) operating in an arena of universality (#9). It is the most success-oriented vibratory force that exists. It has within it the vibrational patterns of the #1 and the #9. The #1 is known as the "Alpha" of numbers while the #9 is the "Omega." The #19 contains within its influence the attributes of all numbers. Wherever that #19 functions, it functions with the multiplicity of all the numbers in the unfolding environment.

Very little can go "wrong," since the protective envelope of each number comes into play when the event or situation calls for it. And even if the person who is "protected" tries to "purposefully" make things go wrong (the person who can't seem to do anything right, or who seems to do things to the contrary even when they know better), they still seem to come up smelling like a "rose." Although that type of person can perhaps, limit or restrict the degree of their success, the #19 still seems to "protect" them from absolute failure.

The number 21 has already been discussed to some extent earlier when discussing the #12. It is also known as the number of entertainment (self expression in the public arena). The number 2 which dominates gives emphasis to cooperation, sensitivity to others and responsiveness, supported by (but not dominated by) the attributes of leadership, individuality and creativity which are inherent in the #1 vibratory influence. This combination of the #2, #1 and the root #3, which sets the tone of the #21 influence, makes the #21 a very magnetic and "entertaining" number.

The number 22, like the #11, is a "Master" number. Its root vibration is the #4. The number 22 is the #4 vibratory force raised up in emphasis and intensity. Where the #4 represents foundation, framework, discipline and detail, the #22 represents the Master Carpenter, the Master Builder, or the Cosmic Mason who is engaged in the laying of a foundation upon which the world can build a much stronger society. The foundation can be physical, social or spiritual. The number 22 builds the road upon which others tread.

The "double" #2 in the number amplifies the intuitive and imaginative faculties of the #2, which are also attributes of the #22. The two #1's of the #11 and the two #2's of the #22, the "doubleness" of the Compound Number's digits, *more* than doubles the intensity of the single digit patterns. The #22 governs things of the earth (through the root #4). People who operate within the vibrational influence of the #22 need to be aware of the necessity to maintain balance between the sensitivity of the #2 and the practicality of the #4.

The number 22 person can make a good bricklayer or carpenter or become the leader of an international "foundation" dedicated to providing the groundwork for others to build upon, particularly if the goal is cooperation between all people. The number 22 would also be a very natural vibrational pattern for a building contractor—whether in building structures or in paving roads. The number 22 vibration has a greater potential for achievement than its root #4, although that is no guarantee that the potential will be realized.

The number 23 is the most fortunate of the #5 root vibrations, and is the second most fortunate number in Numerology, following the #19. It brings together the #2 which is cooperation, partnership and creative imagination, with the #3 which is self expressive, intuitive, and social in nature.

The number 2 dominates, which allows the receptivity of the #2 to provide the channel for bringing "success" to the #23 vibrational patterns, while the "ambitious" #3 gives added strength to this very high potential vibratory force. The best of both influences come together with optimum results, with the overtone of the root #5 patterns. Remember that the #5 is the number of freedom, communications, action and movement.

All of the numbers of the #23 emphasize some aspect of rapport and communications. The number 2 represents cooperation, the #3 represents speaking and the public, while the #5 is the "number" of communications (words in action). Anything dealing with acting, singing, lecturing, selling, public relations, advertising, entertainment (where words and communications are involved) will prosper under the influence of the #23.

The number 25 is the most fortunate of the #7 root vibrations. It is considered a very "spiritual" vibrational pattern. It is known as the number of "prophecy" and intuitive experiencing. It is the sensitivity, receptivity and creative imagination of the #2 operating in the environment of the #5 which brings with it communications, freedom and movement, while the tone of the #25 pattern is set by the vibratory force of the root #7.

The number 7 is the number of the highly-tuned (illumined) intellect, meditative experiencing, introspection, scientific courage and seeking the truth of the reality behind the appearance. The #25 influence enhances spiritual endeavors, is perfect for meditating on or about reality, and increases the anticipation of receiving inner understanding of outer relationships.

The number 27 is the most *spiritually* but not necessarily the most success (material) oriented, of all the numbers. Although it is a fortunate number for certain material happenings and events, it is not a "material" number per se. The root number of the #27 is the #9 which is the number of the metaphysician, healer, humanitarian and sets the tone for the unfolding vibrational patterns of the #27. Added to this influence of the #9 is the influence of the #7 which, being the secondary aspect of the #27, is the tempering or supportive vibration of the parent Compound Number. The number 7 is the number of the mystic, the illumined intellect and the seeker of the truth of reality.

The vibratory forces of the #9 and the #7 make this number 27 very significantly spiritual in effect. These aspects are also combined with the vibrational patterns of the #2 which brings with it sensitivity, creative imagination, receptivity and the "ability" to *see* both sides of an issue, situation or event clearly. The number 27 governs the area of health (whether of body, mind or soul) as well as nursing, medicine, physicians and metaphysicians, healers, surgeons, nutritionists, the "protective" services of a social nature such as police, firemen and the military (the nation's, state's or community's "surgeons").

The significant aspect of the #40 is the phenomenon of the occurrence of the "40 days and 40 nights" as a measure of certain events such as the "Great Flood," and Jesus Christ's time spent in the wilderness when he was being tested for his resolve. The number 40, by virtue of the root #4, represents structure, framework, attention to detail, discipline and completion for establishing a "foundation" for accomplishment. The "zero" gives the #4 a greater pattern of achievement within the environment of the unfolding patterns. The "zero" which represents "potential" in combination with the #4 indicates the completion of a *major endeavor* or major project, or the establishment of a well-developed, detailed plan of action for a major project. Christ spent "40 days and nights" in the wilderness in *preparation* for what he would have to do in the future.

In defining Compound Numbers, once you move beyond the #54, the preponderance of the numbers reduce down to Compound Numbers already discussed in the first 54 in sequence. Above the #54, the interpretation becomes a repetitive process of analysis and evaluation of each of the single digits of the Compound Number in relationship to the other and its root number vibrational patterns.

For instance, the #55 is the "double" 5 which accents the attributes of the #5; it reduces down to the #10 which has already been discussed and related. With the 56, you know the aspects of the #5 and the aspects of the #6; you know that the #5 dominates, being first; the #56 reduces to

#11; the #57 to the #12, etc. You have enough familiarity of the application and technique of interpretation to be able to understand under what conditions and in what circumstances certain vibrational patterns can provide a particular environment for optimum performance.

When you see the #62, you know that it will be similar to the #26, but with slight variations due to the dominance of the #6 instead of the #2. However, both the #62 and the #26 have the root #8 determining the tone of the unfolding patterns. The #63 is similar to the #36, the #64 to the #46 which reduces down to the #10 as does the #55. And so on. As I have said, a repetitive pattern of interpretation develops which allows you to quickly and easily determine the influence of a particular Compound Number in relationship to a current event.

Too many books on Numerology and too many numerologists will state that certain Compound Numbers mean certain things, but fail to give you some understanding as to why the numbers mean what they do and how the definitions are arrived at. I hope that the information and discussion about the Compound Numbers in this chapter will at least give you some insight into the understanding and interpretation of the language of Compound Numbers. It is the Compound Number which gives one an "added" dimension and additional ("between the lines") information about important events in one's life.

READING BETWEEN THE LINES
The Meaning of Compound Numbers

The Number	The Description
10	Zero taken by itself signifies *eternal, universal, source.* Taken in compound with another digit (number) gives the number added dimension, increased potential, "open endedness."

—increases the potential of the #1.

—the inherent ability to lead magnified; enhances honor and prestige.

—success-oriented vibrational pattern (whether for seemingly "good" or "evil" purposes).

—a high vitality vibration which "starts the cycle" of compound numbers.

—spiritually (metaphysically) a return to wholeness.

—significance of the #10 appears as the *Ten Commandments* (Decalog); ten patriarchs of Israel; Genesis 18:33 (in Sodom and Gomorrah)—"if there be '10' there, I will not destroy it"; in the countdown for launching rocketships—10, 9, 8, 7, . . . zero/liftoff.

11   A *Master* number which represents two upright columns that lead into the "temple" of our inner being.

—made up of two "1's" which amplifies the creative originality and individuality of the #1.

—symbolism represents equilibrium or the balance between two extremes.

—it is the number of idealism combined with aspiration.

—it is the #2 raised up or magnified in vibratory force— imagination, romanticism, inventiveness, sensitivity.

—vibrational patterns are charismatic, magnetic, and electrical being keyed to limelight activities.

—psychic, visionary, dreamer.

—intensely emotional; great nervous energy and dramatic flair.

The Number	The Description

—a #11 must be aware that the intellect may attempt to submerge or block the operation of the intuition.

12   Its root number is the 3 which denotes self expression, intuition, and integration (of mind, body, soul).

—the vibrational pattern is made up of the #1 (which dominates since it is "first" in order)—unity, individuality, creativity—as influenced by the #2—cooperation, receptivity, sensitivity, diplomacy.

—the vibrations are balanced and indicate moral and ethical overtones.

—the power of the #12 derives from the "3" which governs the desire to achieve "at-one-ment" of body, mind and spirit.

—favorable environment for reasoning and intellect; great for debates and speaking engagements.

—significance is found in the 12 disciples of Christ; 12 tribes of Israel; 12 sons of Jacob; 12 months of the year; 12 signs of the Zodiac; 12 powers of man; 12 hours/AM to 12 hours/PM.

13   The most abused of all numbers; it is not "unfortunate" as has been supposed for all these ages; its *power* is misunderstood or misinterpreted because of the combination of the #1 and the #3, both of which are "masculine": directive, aggressive and forceful—creativity and individuality reinforce by self expression and ambition. As a result, one may feel "overpowered" by such a high concentration of energy, and be intimidated (unknowingly, of course). However, the #13 still has as its roots the #4 which represents practicality, down-to-earthness, detail, discipline, framework and foundation.

—the vibrational pattern is very structured from its roots and is driven into a "rut" (groove) by the "one way" emphasis of the force of the #1 and the #3, resulting in creativity being stifled.

The Number	The Description

—if used properly, the *power* of the #13 can be directed to build or form many structures and foundations.

—the significance of the #13 can be seen in the "missing" 13th floor of most offices and apartment buildings; the 13th or "lost tribe" of Israel; the 13 original colonies of the United States of America became the "foundation" of America as displayed by the 13 stars and stripes of the first flag; Christ + the 12 disciples.

14

Its root number is the 5 which represents movement, change, action, versatility, and communications (words in action).

—"business oriented" in that the individuality of the #1 is standing on the foundation of a strict set of standards and value structure; however, it is "business" based on action or quick turnaround.

—the number of speculation, such as sales, gambling, real estate, stock market activity.

speculation implies "risk and uncertainty" due to the #5's action and changeability of its vibrational pattern; however, it is not necessarily negative, *if* the risk is seen as a means to excitement and variety in one's experiencing.

—the major significance of the #14 is seen in the book of Matthew of the New Testament of the Bible where it speaks of 14 generations in the historical experience of the people of Israel as the "change" points in their travels; metaphysically speaking, it denotes a time of "change" or "shifting" in each individual's inner experiences.

15

The individual (#1) operating in an environmental pattern of communications, freedom, action and movement (#5).

—considered a number of youthfulness.

—its root #6 brings with it balance, harmony, truth,

The Number	The Description

love, responsibility, teaching, service and family aspects.

—the energy flow that comes from the "I" (#1) in the center of the arena of action (#5) becomes a magnet for financial or material success as well as a "focal point" toward which others are drawn in their need to find help, support or counseling.

16 The #16 represents the individual (#1) operating in an environment of people, community, service and teaching.

—the overview of the #16 is perfection, introspection, intellect, mysticism, faith and "loner" vibrational aspects derived from the root #7.

—the law of preservation rules the #16 and brings with it the desire for continuity, and the use of caution and great care; as a result, the #16 may encourage procrastination.

—the seeming discontent and impatience that may arise from this vibrational influence is most probably due to the "competition" between the #1 which emphasizes individuality and leadership and the #6 which emphasizes devotion to family and service to the community— along with the "loner" aspect of the #7 versus the "up-front" desires of the #1 and the people orientation of the #6.

—favorable environments for the #16 are intellectual, mystical and scientific—anything conducive to seeking the truth of reality.

—this is a good vibrational pattern for educators, editors, and gardners.

17 The #1—creative, original, individual, in conjunction with the #7—mystical, scientific, intellectual, *demands* proof of the validity of things.

—it brings with it the power, judgment, intuition, expansiveness and efficiency of the #8, as well as financial/business/commercial orientation.

The Number	The Description

—it is a number of vitality, courage and ambition which governs large things and affairs.

—carries with it a success-oriented vibrational pattern in banking, insurance, real estate, as an executive for a company or the head of your own business.

—with regard to financial success, it is considered a number of fortune and happiness; this can be derived from the outward flowing and goal-oriented aspects of the #1 tempered by the quiet inner understanding and strength of the #7, while enhanced by the good sense of judgment inherent in the #8.

18

The root #9 represents completion, force, energy, healing, universality, compassion and objectivity.

—the #18 combines the independence of the #1 with the power and efficiency of the #8 as well as the interaction of the leadership vibrations with judgment and intuition.

—it is the number of great leaders associated with either social, political or religious changes and upheavals.

—it is highly emotional and highly intellectual in nature.

—the greatest significance of the #18 lies in the fact that it was the birthname vibration of Jesus Christ, who was responsible for what is probably the greatest religious change in the history of man.

19

The #19 is considered the most "blessed" of all the vibrational patterns; this combination includes the vibrational patterns of all the numbers; it is the beginning (#1) and the ending (#9); the Alpha-Omega number.

—fortune seems to follow this number; with this vibrational pattern in someone's life experience, they could work very hard to make a mess of it, and still be "blessed" with success, even if limited.

—it is the individual (#1) operating in the "universal" (#9) arena, a combination of creation and completion.

The Number	The Description

—governs professions rather than businesses.

—can find success as a musician, politician, aviator, lawyer, as a salesman, electrician or a medical specialist.

20

The "zero" gives an open-ended potential to the qualities of the #2—heightened sensitivity, enriched imagination, magnified receptivity and diplomacy and understanding of the nature of cooperation.

—the #20 is a "natural" peacemaker vibration.

—considered the most fortunate of the #2's.

—many will be attracted to the vibrational pattern of the #20 to receive spiritual, psychological and mental support.

—the pattern of experiences develops from spiritual success and not particularly from material success.

21

The root #3 represents a vibrational pattern of self expression, public activities, social popularity, writing.

—the #21 governs books, publishing and editorial activities as well as being beneficial for dramatics.

—since the qualities of the #2—imagination, sensitivity, receptivity, cooperation—prevail, being "first," the independence, creativity, leadership aspects of the #1 give added strength and forcefulness to the compound #; unlike the #12, the social, imaginative, and creative aspects of this number predominate over the intellectual and structured aspects.

—the receptivity and cooperation of the #2 combined with the individuality and "captaincy" of the #1, make the #21 a highly *magnetic* vibrational pattern.

22

A Master number with the "raised up" or magnified vibratory force of the #4 attributes—where the #4 represents foundation, framework, discipline, and detail—the #22 represents the MASTER BUILDER.

—the double "2" amplifies the intuitive and imaginative faculties of the #2.

The Number	The Description

—operates in a worldwide and international arena.

—the #22 represents the laying of a foundation upon which great humanitarian organizations are built and the paving of roads upon which others will walk and follow.

—governs things of the "earth."

—balance is needed between the sensitive and emotional #2 and the practical #4.

23   Considered the most fortunate of numbers after the #19.

—it brings together the aspects of the #2—cooperation, imagination, partnership, receptivity—and those of the #3—self expression, intuition, public activities, social events.

—the #2, the #3 and its root #5, all emphasize communication, sociability and creative expression—writing, speaking, selling, lecturing, singing, acting, teaching.

—the action, change, freedom, movement and travel aspect of the root #5, in conjunction with the sensitivity of the #2 and the energy-scattering effect of the #3, makes this a "mercurial" vibrational pattern. Solid values and distinct purpose will reap the greatest harvest from this free-flowing vibration.

24   The #2—partnership, in an environment of foundation, #4, as influenced by the #6—family, emphasizes love of home and family.

—the vibrational pattern of the root #6 which emphasizes beauty, balance, harmony, service, along with the receptivity, creative imagination, cooperation and sensitivity of the #2 and the discipline, detail, framework, dependability aspects of the #4 indicates success in people-oriented areas of endeavor, e.g. beauty salons/barber shops, real estate, banking and counseling (anywhere from law to finances).

The Number	The Description

—where the #4 shows up in any combination, a "strictness" of some kind is indicated. Here it indicates a "tightness" of money.

—the harmony of the #6 plus the cooperation of the #2 plus the dependability and loyalty of the #4 makes the #24 vibrational pattern very "magnetic" and will attract attention and generate power by its unfolding possibilities.

25 The most fortunate and the most "spiritual" of the #7's.

—it is the number of "prophecy" and intuitive experiencing; the sensitivity, receptivity and creative imagination of the #2 operating in an environment of freedom, change, movement and words of the #5, blended with the attributes of the root #7—highly tuned intellect, meditative introspection, desire to find the reality behind the appearance.

—the environment of the #25 vibrational pattern enhances and illuminates the comprehension of spiritual principles and mystical experiences.

26 Has the root #8 attributes of power, energy, expansiveness, judgment, executive ability and arena of business/finance/commerce.

—the ability of seeing both sides of the issue (#2) active in an environment of teaching, counseling, service and community (#6) enhanced by the vibrational pattern of the root #8 indicates success in politics, large humanitarian organizations, executive management of your own business.

—the combination of the #2 (partnership) and the #6 (love, family) indicates an early marriage and a long one.

—some seeming conflict may be felt due to the interplay of the sensitivity, cooperation, receptivity vibrations of the #2 and the power, energy and executive authority of the root #8.

The Number	The Description

27 The most "spiritually" oriented of all the numbers.

—it combines the creative imagination and the ability to see both sides of an issue of the #2, the intellectual perception and interest in the "mysterious" aspects of life of the #7, and the vibrational pattern of the root #9—force, energy, healing, universality and objectivity.

—it governs areas of health and medicine, physicians, metaphysicians, healers, surgeons, nutrition, natural foods, military and police.

—an excellent vibration for writing and lecturing on the above.

—the sensitivity of the #2 and the force and energy of the #9 make this an "emotionally" sensitive vibration with a great deal of nervous energy.

28 The creative imagination and sensitive understanding of the #2 operating in an environment of power, energy, judgment, and expansiveness of the #8 within the umbrella vibrational pattern of the root #1—individuality produces a highly effective influence in areas of executive and leadership positions of large organizations and with law, judges and courts.

—can work well with partnerships (#2 dominates).

—can use power and judgment (#8) for making proper changes in course of direction.

—care should be taken to make *wise use* of "judgment" abilities before taking any action.

29 The #29 is the combination of a very "personal" vibrational pattern and a very "impersonal" vibrational pattern, the #2 and the #9. It has "extremist" vibrations as well as intense emotional potential. As a result it has been interpreted as a number to be avoided. However, that is *not* true, since the #2 is accented; being "first" in the compound numbers, it is the dominant and major influence in the unfolding vibrational pattern of the #29.

The Number	The Description

—it's the #2—peacemaker, diplomat, cooperation, partnership, operating in an environment of healing, force, energy and universality, the #9. Add this to the fact that the root vibration is the #2 as well as having the #11 pattern inborn in it, and you will find that the #29 is exciting and charismatic.

—it is very spiritual and inspirational due to the #9 and the #11 pattern potential.

30 All of the possibilities and potential of the #3 vibrational pattern—self expression, intuition, ambition, money, drive—are magnified with the addition of the "zero."

—arena of drama and dramatic expression emphasized, particularly acting: playwriting also indicated (writing and publishing of words aspects).

—it is the number of social life and entertainment.

31 The root vibration #4 produces discipline, detail, structure, routine, loyalty.

—it is the #3 vibrational pattern of self expression, ambition, writing, speaking, socializing operating in an environment of the #1 which is conducive to leadership, the opportunity to pioneer new fields and creative originality.

—the structure of the #4 may tend to limit the potential of the #31, but cannot totally contain it.

—this vibratory influence is conducive to "good business sense" and practicality.

—it is not as powerful as the #13 due to the control of the #3, self expression and integration instead of the #1.

32 Along with the root #5 vibrations of freedom, communications (words in action), the #3—self expression, words (writing, public speaking, lecturing) ambition, social expression—dominates. And although its overall vibrational pattern is very similar to the #23, it is not as

The Number	The Description

balanced and stable as the #23 which has its major influence derived from the #2.

—it is the number of friends, social activities and business connections.

—good vibratory influence for the quick study of different languages.

33 The most favorable of the #6's, it combines the overall vibrational pattern of the root #6—harmony, balance, love, service, teaching, beauty, truth with a magnified influence of the two #3's.

—this "double" three combination emphasizes self expression, is highly ambitious, stresses big business, is a strong "money" number and is very "public" in nature. This emphasis is characterized by both the pattern of the #6 and the pattern of the #3.

—the high concentration of self expression, of ambition, of drive and the power outflow of the double 3's would make it a good number for revolutionaries and for anyone who was challenging concepts, attitudes, dogma and rigid values.

34 The root #7 governs intellect, analytical abilities, desire for knowledge of the "mysterious" aspects of life, meditation and introspection. Within this pattern, the vibratory force of the #3 manifests self expression, intuition, integration in an environment of discipline, foundation, detail and framework of the #4.

—it is finely tuned both "spiritually" and psychically due to the structure of the #4, the intuition of the #3 and the highly tuned intellect of the #7.

—the #4 influence along with the intellectual and analytical aspects of the #7 indicates that a "scientific" career and field of endeavor would be successful.

35 With the root #8 having in it power, judgment, business/financial/commercial patterns, the #3 vibrational

The Number	The Description

pattern of writing, "public" speaking, publishing and the vibrational pattern of the #5 which includes freedom, action, movement, communications indicates a very great emphasis on things "literary" as well as on money.

—with the #3 being first, it dominates so that the fields of public speaking and publishing show great promise and potential for success.

—the forcefulness and ambition of the #3 in conjunction with the "changeability" of the #5 can create a "scattering" of energy and efforts; be constantly aware to use the power of the #8 and its inherent "good judgment" aspects in all decisions.

36

After the #19 and the #23, this is the most success-oriented number in Numerology.

—the most favored of the #9's, it combines the attributes of the #3—self expression, intuition, ambition, with the qualities of the #6—harmony, balance, truth, service, teaching, counseling.

—would govern metaphysical teaching centers, or any center, organization, business which emphasizes creative self-expression, healing or personal counseling.

—it is a good vibrational pattern for "teaching" hospitals, medical referral or consultation business.

37

This number not only has the root #1 vibration—individuality, leadership, pioneering, creative originality, but also has the #10 inherent in it with all its potential for success.

—the #3 brings drive, intuition, outgoingness, public vibrations into combination with the #7 vibrational pattern—highly tuned intellect, meditative and introspective attributes, and the desire to seek the reality behind the appearance.

—the #3 is the number of entertainment, friendship, so-

The Number	The Description

cial popularity and is enhanced by the gregariousness of the root #1.

—governs businesses and events which entertain the public.

38 Within the #38 is the #11 (3 + 8) as well as the root vibrational pattern of the #2.

—here the #3 is a very "strong" masculine number of *self expression*, ambition, and *intuition* operating in an environment of the #8—a very "strong" feminine number of power, judgment, intuition. Add to this the innate qualities of the #11 and you have a very *spiritually* powerful vibrational pattern.

—this power vibration has been misinterpreted and misunderstood; this has been caused by the seeming conflict between the #3 vibration—masculine, directive, active and the #8 vibration—feminine, receptive, passive, a misconception derived from one looking at these vibrations as opposite or opposing one another. They are not opposites but rather complements.

—highly intuitive, highly charismatic and psychic in nature.

39 Contains within it the #12 vibrational pattern as well as the #3 root vibrational pattern.

—emphasis is on self expression, intuition, integration inherent in the #3 as dominating the compound number (being first), in the #12 and in the root vibration as functioning in an environment of the #9—healing, metaphysics, medicine, universal precepts and objectivity.

—writing, lecturing, expressing in relation to the #9 activities is indicated.

40 Magnification of the attributes of the root #4—discipline, hard work, loyalty, method, detail, routine, framework and foundation; the influence of the zero as representing potential and choice gives a greater pattern of achievement relative to the function of the #4.

The Number	The Description

—indicates completion of a major endeavor; such as the "laying of a foundation," in both the physical and metaphysical sense; the establishment of a well-defined plan of action.

—significance of the #40 is shown in the 40 days and nights of the Great Flood in the Old Testament before Noah and the Ark found land upon which to start the race anew; and the 40 days and nights that Jesus Christ spent in the "wilderness" preparing, planning and deciding on a course, prior to his getting about the business of completing his mission (see the #18 and the #9).

41 Similar to the #14, except that with the #4 coming first reduces the "risk" involved because of the structure and foundation aspects of the #4 having the greater impact, as influenced by the attributes of the #1—individuality, leadership, creativity.

42 Similar to the #24 vibrational pattern, except with the #4 coming first and dominating, implies a *potentially* "strict code" of values shaping the environmental patterns unfolding.

—indicates a religious overtone in the sense of dogma, creed, established set of values.

—significance of the #42 seen in the reference to the 42 generations from Abraham to the birth of Christ as mentioned in the Book of Matthew, first chapter.

43 The discipline, detail, routine of the #4 in an environment of the #3 patterns of expression, drive, ambition tend to influence military activities, particularly in connection with revolution, upheavals of any kind and preventative action.

—the overtone of the root #7 attributes still governs things spiritual, scientific and intellectual.

44 The double 4 emphasizes practicality, loyalty, discipline, sticktuitiveness. This is in connection with the root #8—power, energy, judgment governs success in

The Number	The Description

pursuit of a military career as well as success in any practical undertaking.

45 A success-oriented number which governs the helping of others and involvement in the upliftment of the race consciousness (the root #9).

—the #4 dominates and indicates preparing for the action of the #5 in an overall vibrational pattern of its root #9—universality, healing, force, energy.

—the #5 implies that "communications" skills will play an important part in the success of action taken.

46 Combines the practicality of the #4 with the idealism of the #6, while still having the attributes of the root #1 and the #10—pioneering spirit, leadership abilities, creativity.

—it stands for framework, foundation, builder (#4) operating in an environment of balance, family, service, community, truth, beauty.

—when "foundation" *rules* "idealism," great works are accomplished.

47 Combination of the discipline, method, routine of the #4 with the intellectual and analytical abilities of the #7 give this compound number special significance for scientific endeavors.

—with the vibrational patterns of the root #2, and the #11 also inherent in the #47, this creates an interweaving environment of discrimination (#4), cooperation (#2), visionary ideas (#11) and analysis (#7).

48 The root #3 vibrational patterns of self expression, *intuition,* and integration, along with the vibrational patterns of the #8—power, judgment, *and* intuition magnify the psychic and prophetic aspects of being/experiencing.

—the practicality, hard work and framework aspects of the #4 dominate, and in combination with the social

The Number	The Description

and public attributes of the #3 governs things that are down-to-earth.

—success generated through joining of intuition with practicality.

49

This number is discipline, foundation and framework operating in an environment of healing, high energy, force and universality (#9); the "power" of the #13 inherent in the #49 and the force of the #9 are balanced by the fact that the root vibrational pattern of the #4 gives structure and form to the environment.

—governs the laying of a foundation in areas related to the healing of body, mind, and soul.

50

The "zero" magnifies and intensifies the impact of the root #5 vibrational patterns.

—accelerated action, major changes, rapid movement, broadened freedom and multiple experiences.

51

Communications, movement, action, change and freedom (#5) "rule" this compound number, but with pioneering (new ideas, new associations), leadership, individuality and creative originality of the #1 providing a supporting role.

—governs such areas as investigative reporting, detective work.

—the root #6 vibrational pattern of harmony, beauty, balance, calmness and truth provides a protective umbrella over any action which occurs under the influence of the #51.

52

The action of the #5 vibration in combination with the creative imagination and "seeing" both sides of an issue aspect of the #2, plus the intellectuality, analytical aspect and the truth seeking aspect of the #7 makes this Compound Number a good influence for finishing up, tying up loose ends and completing projects.

—significance seen in the 52 weeks in a year.

The Number	The Description
53	Same as the #35, except that public relations, promotional sales, advertising arenas would benefit the most, since the #5 (words in action) is first, it rules the vibration of the #53.
54	The #4 gives stability to the "action" of the #5.

—communications operating from a strong foundation and detailed plan.

—success indicated in promoting compassion and healing (#9) to the world.

11
Soul Qualities Development
Fulfilling the Cycle of Your Experience

When there are certain numbers missing from the spelling of your birthname, it is an indication of things left undone. It points to those qualities which you consciously chose not to express, develop or experience in a past reality (historically speaking). These qualities are called Soul Qualities and are sometimes referred to as "Karmic Lessons." The process by which we "fill" in the "missing" numbers is known as *Soul Qualities Development*. This area of Soul Qualities Development gives us a clue as to where we are in our understanding and evolvement and how close we are to the point of moving on to the next highest level of experiencing. If there are three or more missing numbers in the numbers of the letters of our name, then it normally indicates a very young soul or an old soul who is very stubborn.

The more we pay attention to the areas we need to resolve, the greater the joy in completing our experience. It is important to remember that these unresolved areas are so because of *our* decisions *not* to experience such qualities previously. Proper attention can give one insight into the value of knowing what we didn't do. Therefore, by knowing what we should concentrate on, we can now focus on those specifics which will bring a fuller satisfaction to our experiencing.

One of the more interesting aspects of Soul Quality Development is that our environmental patterns key us toward development of these qualities to their fullest extent, almost pushing us beyond our limits.

Therefore, on an inner level, we are keyed to take *full* advantage of all the opportunities presented to us to bring about the understanding and integration of the qualities for which we are in "training." We may, as a result, end up becoming quite stubborn (sometimes fanatical) about certain kinds of things in our lives which we are "holding" onto, thinking we know that there can be no other "right" concept.

Let's look at the significance of the vibrational pattern of the #7 "Soul Quality Development" environment. The language of the #7 indicates that an environment of study, science, knowledge and philosophy is the best or "optimum" environment for experiencing the necessary facets required to attain this Soul Quality. What then happens is that as a child, we will tend to lean toward things scientific, religious or mathematical and could become quite studious—for the #7 seeks to find out the meaning of things physical as well as metaphysical and to learn about the reality behind the appearance.

Where this leads the child—scientist, engineer, mathematician, philosopher or minister—will depend on how the environment unfolds and the impact of the child's choices of companions and study habits, of reaction to responses of its peers, leaders, heroes, etc. Success or failure will be keyed around whether one wishes to *fully* express their "inner awareness" or only to pay lip service to the nature of their potential.

The number 7 indicates a prior *unwillingness* to train one's mind in a logical and scientific manner. The concentration of the child's first years on developing its mind may even lead it (when an adult) to one day question its preoccupation with the logical or scientific approach to things. Whenever you get *in tune* with the Soul Quality environmental patterns you may become so deeply involved in those experiences that you may treat other equally significant patterns with less importance. This could divert you from the primary direction of your blueprint.

However, at some juncture, a major change will occur in your living patterns which starts you moving on a course that will bring you to a point of understanding the process of experiencing all of the aspects of your being. When this occurs, you will be able to see the value of fulfilling the "requirements" of the particular Soul Qualities.

One aspect of the #7 says that one must learn to examine causes before coming to conclusions—ergo logic, science, math, or exactness of knowledge. However, another aspect of the #7 calls for the discipline of discovering "metaphysical" and "spiritual" understanding and application, in other words, having "faith." One will be "given" the opportunity to develop *faith* as a replacement for trust in things and reliance on people or anything else that is worldly, material, physical and scientific. I defined faith as the operation of an inner power which provides intuitive or direct knowing of *what* must be done, *what* method can be used for the quickest and most successful approach and *which* direction will bring your greatest fulfillment.

Once logic, planning, method and science are understood (i.e. using one's mind), then the power of the mind, in and of itself, is no longer fruitful as the primary initiative in your life. You are placed in situations or environments where you will now be required to act on "faith," letting logic develop the *details* of the move rather than determining the direction of your experiencing.

Once you start operating on "faith," you will discover that you will not have to be caught up in planning (or rather "pre-planning") the details of your life. You begin to take things as they come, letting your mind, and your logical approach to things help you to clear the way, then that faith will yield immediate and continuous results.

The reason that I have discussed the meaning behind the #7 in such depth is to give you an idea of how to evaluate or *interpret* a particular vibrational pattern. This process of understanding the language behind the Soul Quality numbers is a part of the overall VIA (Vibrational Interpretive Analysis) process. It can better allow you to realize the potential scope of VIA as an important contribution to the value that can be derived from the language of numbers.

As you learn to understand the language of your Soul Quality numbers, whole new vistas will present themselves. You can begin to see yourself reach a point in your own envolvement where the development of *all* the Soul Qualities is being completed. You can flow with your experiences and grow and profit by the lessons learned. And, instead of having to *search* for fulfillment, you can begin to let your experiences *come to you* as your life is fulfilled.

SOUL QUALITIES DEVELOPMENT

These are "qualities" which need to be developed in order to bring about balance, harmony and equilibrium in your experiencing, not only in this life environment, but also for filling out the sum total of all of your realities as a completed experiential cycle.

The qualities which need development are found by discovering which vibrational patterns are *lacking* in the letters of your name at birth. Set your name across a page and assign the proper numerical values underneath each letter. (See the Chaldean System assignment in Chapter 2)

W I L L I A M   P H I L L I P   M I K E

6 1 3 3 1 1 4   8 5 1 3 3 1 8   4 1 2 5

Make a table to show how many of each "number" you have in your name.

# 1's	=	6		# 5's	=	2
# 2's	=	1		# 6's	=	1
# 3's	=	4		# 7's	=	NONE
# 4's	=	2		# 8's	=	2

Above, there are no 7's, indicating that it is an area which was consciously "avoided" in the past. It defines the nature of the lessons in life which will opportunely present themselves throughout the total life experience.

SOUL QUALITIES DEVELOPMENT
Vibrational Descriptions

The Number	The Description
1	Not willing to confront issues firmly with resolve.

—failure in believing your own inner power

—shirking of "leadership" opportunities

—lack of courage; overly cautious; indecisive

—uses delay tactics in beginning new projects

—you may have to *fight* for your "place in the sun" until the qualities of the #1 are realized; when that occurs, you will be able to express your "individuality" naturally

The Number	The Description

2

Dislike and avoidance of detail and obedience.

—impatient, tactless, lacking in diplomacy

—considered "time" and keeping of appointments as unimportant

—missed the "trees for the forest"

—will need to develop great patience and pay attention to detail; you may find yourself trimming hedges (figuratively speaking), pruning trees, or climbing many steps in your walk to the top

3

Indicates a failure to promote yourself when the occasion requires it.

—lack of self confidence and self esteem

—avoided any form of self expression

—evaded and hid from public and social events

—you will find yourself in experiences, situations, events where the qualities of self expression such as lecturing, speaking, writing and possibly singing will be required for success

4

Avoided hard work, discipline, orderliness in favor of ease, comfort, luxury and slovenliness.

—you missed the value of the #4 attributes i.e., the concept of "laying a foundation"

—took shortcuts and paths of least resistance

—learn to establish your life's foundation through slow, steady, careful work and discipline

5

Avoided life experiences in general, and particularly with other human beings.

—lacked understanding, versatility and adaptability

—made an effort to avoid anything new and innovative

—you will experience constant change, and may be placed in many emergency situations

—you must be more "worldly" in order to profit from the lesson of freedom and action

The Number	The Description

6
—shows a prior refusal to assume responsibility
—you displayed a fear of being tied down, performing duties and fulfilling obligations
—failed to understand the beauty of service to people
—events will place you in an environment where family and friends will require support and care
—must learn to adjust, adapt and respond
—meeting your obligations will be very important

7
Indicates a prior decided unwillingness to train your mind in a logical and scientific manner.

—failure to examine causes before coming to conclusions or accepting results
—avoided inner or spiritual development
—you will be given the opportunity to develop "faith" as a replacement for trust in things and reliance on people
— you will strive to learn the difference between illusion and reality

8
Avoided things material and physical.
—lacked courage in financial dealings; feared risks of speculation
—doubted own abilities in handling financial transactions; showed poor judgment and carelessness in money matters
—learn to be your own boss and to operate your own business
—you may experience the loss of a great deal of money in order to feel its lack until the lesson of wisdom and judgment shows you the proper use and distribution of *your* own funds

12
Compatibility

The Nature of the Personal Connection

Through the language of each person's numbers, you can find out how compatible you are with someone by looking at "connections."

Can two people work well together—for a long time, for a short time? And, what environments or situations are best suited to each? You can look at the aspects of a relationship and see where each person is in tune with the other. And you need only look at the four "basic" aspects of their numbers.

Your total name at birth is your Purpose or Mission, also known as your calling, your "intuitive" perspective. Your vowels show you your Heart's Desire, your "emotional" perspective. Your consonants give you your Personality, "as others see you," your "physical" perspective. The language of your birthdate is your Destiny, life path or reality cycle, your "intellectual" perspective.

When setting up a compatibility chart, you should automatically get a description of each of the aspects for each person involved so that you can find their connections (See Illustration 12a.). You look at the language of each of their numbers and focus on their "intuitive" viewpoints (inner or spiritual attraction), their "emotional" viewpoints (emotional or psychological attraction), their "physical viewpoints (not only mutual physical attraction, but also attraction to particular things and environments), and their "intellectual" viewpoints (philosophical, mental, ethical attraction—how one thinks about the world).

Many people get together because their consonants are in "tune," which is purely "physical." The "personality" and "outer image" one projects attracts the "personality" and "outer image" of another. There is an almost immediate liking and "seeming" rapport, the beginning of a strong physical relationship.

However, physical attraction is the weakest connection of all the aspects in regard to establishing a "meaningful and lasting" relationship. The weakness is primarily due to the fact that the "personality" is only a role that is being played at a particular time. It can be "changed" deliberately, from the necessity of experience, or because of the growth and expansion of one's perspective of life.

Your personality includes how you see your environment, the city where you live, the home in which you reside, the job in which you find yourself, the people whom you have befriended, any experience with which your "personality" acts, reacts and interacts.

To discover how compatible two people are, you take each individual's birthname and birthdate and work their numbers out into a chart format (See Illustration 12a.). The numbers identify the aspects which will be compared between two other people or between you and another person.

If all or most of the vibrational patterns or potential environments are the same, a very strong attraction is likely to develop. Far too many times it gives rise to a situation which indicates a "potentially" closed (too tight) relationship and as a result limits each one's creative expression. By knowing this, you can be conscious of the possibility of *too* many "like" interests. Then you can allow a variety of experiences to unfold and provide a stimulating and exciting relationship.

The same thing is also true in the opposite sense, where you have all of the numbers between each person reflect "opposing" vibrational patterns. Initially a strong attraction could develop, because of the "diversity" of interests and potential variety in the relationship.

Be aware that if the differences are "too" great (too few like interests), one or the other person may end up disliking the experience. However, if the relationship is of importance to you, your understanding will allow you to adapt and adjust much more easily to the situation and events.

In the determination of compatibility, look for a balance of potential experiences. A balance of interests, aspirations, drive and motivation occurs when there are two or three "major" connections between two people. A major connection is present, when one person's "vowels"—Heart's Desire, emotional perspective, how one feels—is in tune with another's vowel's. The same is true between total birthnames (intuition), total birthdates (intellectual), between vowels and birthname or birthdate, and between the birthname and birthdate. This results in an inter-rapport between two major unfolding vibrational patterns which are a natural point of sharing.

When you are working with someone or are having a personal relationship with someone, and there seems to be something that's not quite right, some "troubling aspect" that's hard to pinpoint, setting up a compatibility chart can give you insight as to what the problem might be and the solution.

And you can even go further than this. You can compare each person's Pinnacles, Challenges, and Personal Years. These can be an aid in understanding underlying influences that will have an important effect on the unfolding patterns of each person involved. You can then become aware of "potential" channels or roadblocks that may influence the flow of rapport between two people.

If you choose, you can take 9 or 10 aspects of your patterns or another person's patterns of experiencing and develop a more detailed "compatibility" comparison. You can literally take a look at the unfolding patterns of action that are taking place or are about to take place. You have an opportunity to interpret the language of numbers of the interrelationship between differing vibrational influences, coming together at a specific "period" of time, in a particular location in space.

Of the four major aspects, the physical (consonants) is the aspect which has the most immediate attraction, although by itself it is the weakest link. The next most "attractive" aspects are the emotional and intellectual which are stronger bonds than the physical.

The intellectual aspect represents the way in which you perceive your view of the world around you. Remember it is your intellect which develops your models of life and the things which you worship and pursue. However, it is the emotions which keep you hooked to those models and the objects you worship.

The strongest attraction of all is the intuitive. It is also the least understood aspect. Its inherent strength is derived from the fact that we (intellectual, emotional and physical) *cannot* interfere with its unfolding patterns as they move out from the "inner" circle of our experiencing. Therefore, when that connection is made, it is a very strong, valuable and binding connection. This intuitive bond is so strong that it will operate to maintain a relationship (which may seem weak on the surface) until the two people get their "acts" together. However, the intuitive connector may indicate that a "separation" is of greatest value to both people who may "need" to be in new environments.

Each of the four major aspects taken by themselves is, of course, still only one part of the whole. Let yourself "see" as much of the whole as possible, so that you can make the best determination as to the nature of any relationship you are considering.

Do not look for a compatibility chart which will "make" a relationship work. Look for one that will "allow" a relationship to work. Understanding the language of your numbers and the numbers of others can provide you with a means of developing more meaningful and lasting relationships.

ILLUSTRATION 12a

Compatibility Determination

Source of the Number	The Aspect	The Attraction	The Numbers of A	B
I. Full Name at Birth (Chapter 2)	Purpose, Mission	Intuitive, Spiritual	9	6
II. Birthname Vowels (Chapter 3)	Heart's Desire	Emotional, Psychological	6	11/2
III. Birthname Consonants (Chapter 4)	Personality, Outer You	Physical, Personal	3	22/4
IV. Full Birthdate (Chapter 5)	Destiny, Life Cycle	Intellectual, Mental	8	6

NOTE: The underlined numbers indicate points of major connection and influence.

In the relationship shown above, A is the female and B is the male. Both are natural counselors (the #6). A is a "writer"; B is a "speaker." A is the executive, the director (the #8 and #9), while B is the administrator, and teacher (the #6 emphasis).

In this relationship, B's spiritual and intuitional motivation (I. above) is the #6 and is directly in tune with A's emotional viewpoint (II. above). This is a *major* connection. Also an additional bond exists between A's *feelings* about life (II. above) and the way B *thinks* about his life (IV. above), another *major* connection. B can put into words what A feels, while A can help B relate to those feelings.

The number 6 is the "most" compatible of numbers. It is dual in nature, being the number of balance, harmony, adjustment and beauty. The number 6 also represents truth and service to family and community.

In *normal* circumstances, the language of A's "Purpose" (I. above), as defined by the number *9,* would indicate "opposing" vibrations to B.

The number *9* (odd), is forceful and emotional in nature while the number *6* (even) is receptive and calm. However, the "opposition" does not occur in this instance, since the *6* is in *harmony* with all numbers. Therefore, the patterns of A's *9* are compatible with the patterns of B's *6*. Since this connection is not between *equal* numbers, it is minor in nature, although it does *add* to strength of this relationship.

Similarly, the connection between the vowels (II. above) as well as the connection between the birthdates (IV. above) are influenced by the *6*. However, in the vowel (emotional) connection, there is a normal attunement between the balanced *6* and the cooperative *2* (the root of the number *11), which are both even* numbers. In the birthdate (intellectual) connection, A's intuitive *8* allows for an "even" exchange of interests with B's *6*. In this comparison, both the vowels and birthdate numbers, although minor connections, still *add* to the strength of the relationship.

The only "connection" which has a *detracting* effect on this relationship is that of the consonants. A's "physical" viewpoint is keyed around the number *3* (odd). The number *3* is dynamic, energetic, social and ambitious, whereas B's number *4* (even) is methodical, detailed, disciplined and practical. In the beginning, this relationship was erratic, argumentative, sometimes threatening and constantly in conflict. There almost always seemed to be "opposing" personality "snags" that took time and perseverance to straighten out.

However, the strength and importance of the other aspects of this relationship eventually brought about a natural dissolution of any conflict and friction. The spiritual, emotional and intellectual bonds allowed each person to "see through" the personality clash and develop a lasting and creative relationship.

When you make any comparisons, you will from time to time, find that a relationship may not be "ideal." You may not find a strong bond existing. This does not mean that you cannot experience joy and satisfaction in the relationship. For knowing the "potential" between two people can alert you to any conflicting aspects, while allowing you to strengthen the patterns which can take the relationship more into a shared alliance and experience.

13
Miscellaneous Numbers
Names, Addresses, Licenses and Cities

Personal Names

Name changes are made every day, and people don't realize the significance of the changes. This is especially true for women. There is a great deal of "identity" lost when women marry and accept the husband's name as can be attested to by the "second" place women have been given, and by the second-class positions in which women have found themselves.

When a woman accepts a man's last name *as hers* the vibratory patterns that begin to envelop her come as a result of the change in name value which alters her basic name patterns. In other words, the woman accepts a "different" environment (or role) than the one which is "natural" *to her* and *for her* from the time she was born. The "change in name" puts a "veil" around a woman's own unfolding patterns and causes them to become delayed, distorted or diluted.

When a woman divorces and "takes" back her birthname, or simply uses her birthname again, good things begin to happen. Some think this is due to freedom from the marriage. However, it is not the marriage which represses the woman, but her inability to express naturally. Within a short time after a woman begins to work within the framework of her own name (obviously, this can happen without divorce or separation), she begins to feel like a "new" person.

When you change your name, it can have an effect on the events of your life. If the change is in tune with your birthname vibrations, then additional doors will open up for you. If the change in vibrational patterns pulls you away from the basic expression of your natural environment, then success may be limited, or things may be delayed. You may feel restricted in what you are able to do.

If you must change your name, then aim toward keeping the vibrational pattern of your total birthname as part of the new name vibrational pattern. This lets the new name vibration stay in "tune" with the major aspects of the birthname. For if you change the vibrational pattern of your numbers, you may distort or dampen the unfolding patterns of your calling or Purpose as revealed in your name at birth.

(NOTE: If you wish to change your name to match a "new image" or to fit a role you are playing, be sure that you first know and understand the nature of your personal "blueprint." In that way, you can always operate from your own center no matter what "name" you use.)

PERSONAL NAME CHANGES

(1) PRIME DIRECTIVE: Don't change your name unless you *feel* you must. Use and maintain *your name at birth!!*

This has within it three of the four major aspects of the vibrational blueprint of your life experience.

(2) IF THAT'S NOT POSSIBLE: Then try to use a name which will maintain your Total Name *Number,* Your Vowel *Number,* and your Consonant *Number.*

This contains the basis for your intuitional, emotional and physical perspective re: your life experiences.

(3) IF THAT'S NOT POSSIBLE: Then try to maintain your *Total* Birthname *Number.*

This reflects your Intuitional Perspective, your Purpose in life.

(4) IF YOU CAN'T HANG ON TO (1), (2), or (3) above, or you don't want to, then at least know the nature of your own reality and the direction of your experiences given to you by your name at birth.

(5) IF YOU WISH TO CHANGE YOUR "personality," the "first impression" you make, the way others see you, you can set up a new

"image" of yourself *by changing the vibrations of your consonants.* This should help you in developing new associations or in starting anew in a "different" arena.

SET UP A COMPATIBILITY CHART FOR *YOURSELF!!* (See Chapter 12)

(a) Calculate the numbers of your name at birth.
(b) Develop a list of "different" names you may want to use.
(c) Calculate the numbers of the "different" names.
(d) Compare the aspects of the potential new name to your birthname numbers.

Business Names

If you wish to test the potential patterns of a *Business Name,* first determine what you want the business to represent. Do you want your business name to vibrate to "you," or the names of partners; or do you want the business name to vibrate to what the business is?

Set up a compatibility chart and analyze it. Be aware not to distort the spelling of the business name in order to "make it fit" the vibrational pattern you have chosen. Let the "natural" or accepted spelling determine its own vibration. If the name you have "chosen," does not fit the vibrational pattern you wish to develop for your business, *perhaps* the name you have chosen is not the "right" one. If so, keep looking.

If you are an "employee" you can check the name of the company you work for and take a look at its vibrational pattern vs. yours. This is also true for a company you may be interviewing with for a job. Is the company's image compatible to your pattern?

Addresses

The most important thing about selecting addresses is that the "numbers" of the address should be "in tune" with either 1) your Purpose Number, 2) your Heart's Desire, or 3) your Destiny Number, if you wish to take advantage of the most favorable influences. Your greatest ease of living will normally occur when your "home" address is "in tune" with one of the three aspects above. If you live in an apartment, the primary vibrational pattern is determined from your *apartment* (your "home") number, *not* the apartment building street address. The street address simply provides an "overtone" which is secondary to the "number" of your "home."

Licenses

If you would like to make some interesting discoveries, look at the numbers of your automobile license plate and the numbers of your drivers' license. The "numbers" on the license plate provide the basic patterns which surround your car at all times. The vibrational influence of the letters in your license plate number is very minor, unless the license number is all "letters." If that is the case, then you must find the vibrational pattern by assigning the proper numerical value to each letter. (See Chapters 2, 3 and 4 which discuss the birthname numbers.)

Since your car is your present "vehicle" through life, the most favorable vibration would be set up when the license plate number was "in tune" with your birthname number. Second best is the number of your vowels (emotions), while close behind is the number of your birthdate (intellect). Whatever the "number" of your car is, read the definition of any Compound Numbers (Chapter 10) for the nature of the vibrational pattern which affects the environment of your car.

Your drivers' license number is important, since you use it all of your adult life. It gives you, under the law, permission to operate vehicles for your transportation through life. And while you may have several "vehicles" during your lifetime, you usually have only one driver's license. Determine the Compound Number of your driver's license number and discover the language of the vibrational pattern which flows out from it.

You can determine the "number" of *any* type of license which you carry and find it's underlying pattern and influence.

Cities

In determining the "compatability" of yourself and the city where you live, develop the numbers of the city: the purpose, the vowels, and the consonants. You then compare your own vibrational patterns, including Destiny Number, to those of the city to find the interaction between you. If the vibrations of the city match either your Total Name Number, your Destiny Number, or your Vowel Number (in that order of importance and influence), then you will find that you can acclimate yourself to that city very easily and very well. If you only match to the number of your consonants, you will discover that you will find the city exciting at first, but very boring after awhile, even uncomfortable. You may also find yourself gravitating to a city that is in tune to the particular pinnacle in which you find yourself. However, after the pinnacle passes, you may decide to move on unless there is an additional tie to that city.

I've worked out the numbers of the following cities for your convenience. It's interesting to note the character of some of the major ones like London (4), which is practical, dependable, determined; Los Angeles

(11) which is a limelight number, very public and upfront, and Las Vegas (7) which is considered a "lucky" number with intuitive and protective forces.

	Los Angeles	New York	Chicago
Total Name:	11	10/1	23/5
Vowels:	9	6	9
Consonants:	11	4	5

	Philadelphia	Las Vegas	New Orleans
Total Name:	45/9	16/7	15/6
Vowels:	9	7	9
Consonants:	9	9	6

	Denver	Dallas	Miami
Total Name:	27/9	15/6	11
Vowels	1	2	3
Consonants:	8	4	8

	London	Tokyo	Paris
Total Name:	31/4	21/3	15/6
Vowels:	5	6	2
Consonants:	8	6	4

	Rome	Hong Kong	Acapulco
Total Name:	18/9	37/1	32/5
Vowels:	3	5	6
Consonants:	6	5	8

14
Putting Your Act Together
The Numero-Log

The concept of the "Numero-log" (diary of your personal numbers) includes the interrelationship of the major patterns of your experiencing that make up your life. The "Numero-Log" becomes the place where you put all your separate parts together and allow yourself to view your total blueprint. It will include individual sections for each of your major aspects—with the specific "number" and the "language" of that particular aspect.

It will have a section for the language of your total Birthname, your Vowels, your Consonants and your total Birthdate. It will also include sections for your Pinnacles, your Challenges, your Personal Years and Personal Month Vibrations and your Goal Power Number. There will be follow-up sections which I call "appendices." Each appendix will be the basis for putting groupings of aspects together so that you will be able to see a broader picture of your life's potential.

The Numero-Log is Numerology without the *Y* (why?). It is the why answered. It is a record of your "journey" through this life of experiences. The "Log" will not only provide the descriptions of the most important aspects of your blueprint, but will also provide sections that have a number of "supporting" aspects. The miscellaneous sections of the Numero-Log will include, among other things, a place for name changing, Soul Qualities Development, selection of a business name, compatibility comparisons, etc.

Numerology, the science of numbers, indicates that there are certain number values which represent sound vibrations. These sound vibrations are keyed to our phonetic alphabet and to the various *sounds* of the letters and/or combinations of letters. Each of these number values has a definition in terms of the language we use and the aspect under consideration. But that's as far as Numerology goes. It gives you words that correspond to number values. It does not provide the means of understanding the language behind those numbers and the connections which will give you an overview of your life's blueprint.

Although I use the science of numbers and the numerological techniques needed to calculate the number values of the different aspects, I do not stop there. It is not only numbers which I work with, but also the language behind the numbers. My emphasis is on the *language* of numbers and the interpretation and translation of that language which is what I call *Numerolinguistics*. It defines the overall concept which underlies the work in this book.

Numerolinguistics translates the vibrational behavior of numbers into written symbols and meaningful patterns. It does not limit the discussion of numbers to the individual aspects. It expands the discussion to include the interrelationships which are needed to define the blueprint for experiencing. The individual aspects and the interrelationships of your numbers are brought together in the Numero-Log.

Your numbers are significant parts of the same whole, all pieces of a puzzle which only you can complete. It may be interesting to know your Destiny by itself or your Mission by itself, but what if there are seeming conflicts in your vibrations. You would want to know if they are reconciliable, since all of those aspects express your potentiality.

What if you have a #5 Destiny, which is communications, movement, freedom and action, and a number 7 Mission—which is an inner number, a number of withdrawal, of the intellect, very analytical? The number 5 is very outward going, while the #7 is quite inward looking. How does one reconcile the differing feelings and drives?

You don't have to reconcile anything. Instead of having to cope with life, you can start living it. Bring the best of each of the aspects of your being into play and let them work together as your life unfolds into what you are. Let the patterns which give you the most out of life be woven into their proper place in the scheme of your experiencing.

Each number's symbols and patterns define specific influences, environmental possibilities, events, situations and potential experiences. Your Numero-Log brings your series of patterns together and gives you a set of potentials and possibilities from which to choose. You can also choose the time or times that certain actions can or will take place. You supply the variations, choose the arena where you want to "perform" and act out the scenes you've prepared to the audience you want to perform in front of.

A person with a strong #8 influence may be deeply involved in banking, or be a judge, both of which are natural to the #8. The careers or "arenas" here may be very different while at the same time, very natural to the #8. The "naturalness" is due to the *intuitive ability* inherent in the #8 vibration which makes the #8 an excellent judge of money, people, circumstances, events, etc.

You will find that seeming differences are not really differences when you understand each number's root meaning. The nature of the root identity of numbers is discussed at length in Chapter 10 on Compound Numbers. For instance, #18 has the root of the #9 (1 plus 8). Therefore the #9 has a very strong influence on the meaning of the #18. But the #18 vibrational pattern is also dependent on the #1 and the #8 as part of the unfolding environment, a vibrational pattern which comes off the second number, and the "combined" (interwoven) pattern which flows from the #18 and is focused around the pattern of the root #9.

It is like tossing a pebble into the center of a pond and watching the concentric circles flow out from the point of impact of the pebble. You and I are that pebble. This physical experience is the pond. Numerolinguistics is the *means* to finding the patterns that are flowing out from the point of contact you have with your experiences. Your life unfolds as you experience each "concentric" circle and expands into ever-increasing circles which are moving out from your center. Your Numero-Log is the place where you *record* your patterns.

It gives you a distinct view and direction for this particular life experience. The pattern or the symbols of the pattern that come out of your blueprint can help you make decisions because it shows you the areas which are going to be the most fruitful for you and where you can find your greatest success or fulfillment. You can now take a look at what kind of outer framework you want for the house that your blueprint is building for you. You can move from trying to find out what you want—to taking the necessary action that will bring you what you know is yours.

How many times have you asked yourself, "What is the right action for me?" Or "What's the right direction for me to take?" And "What should I do in order to get things right the first time instead of having to do things over again?" Your Numero-Log sets down the guidelines for making the choices, which can lead you to right results. You will have an awareness as to what is happening, what is about to happen or what can potentially happen. You can achieve a greater sense of satisfaction in your life, as you learn to "resonate" to your own patterns of experiencing.

You permit yourself to get in tune with those things that are natural to you, instead of trying to make your life and your experiences "fit" some model you thought was right. You will find that you no longer have to "program" yourself with some cure-all technique, reprogram yourself with more so-called "positive" values, or develop a set of "affirmations" to carry you through the day. You will discover that you no longer have to make things happen, you now *let* things happen.

You already know who you are. Every day that you awaken proves that you are aware for you cannot be aware of the day without being aware of yourself first. That is your true starting point. The information which you put together in your Numero-Log sets the pattern and provides the foundation for defining that starting point. Once you begin to assimilate this understanding, then the rest of experiencing is a matter of enjoyment.

YOUR "NUMERO-LOG"
Putting Your Act Together

This is a diary of your personal numbers. It is no one else's, nor can it be. It is your life; this is your record; it is your journey.

Section 1
FULL NAME AT BIRTH*
Purpose/Mission
(Intuitive Perspective)

BIRTHNAME: W I L L I A M   P H I L L I P   M I K E

ALPHABET/NUMBERS: 6 1 3 3 1 1 4   8 5 1 3 3 1 8   4 1 2 5

               19   29   12

               10   11   3

               1 plus 11 plus 3 equals 15

               1 plus 5 equals 6

BIRTHNAME NUMBER: 6

"Doing unto others as you would have them do unto you." Cosmic parent or teacher; responsibility and trust. Music and theater arts are natural. A strong influence for harmony and beauty in every environment. Inspiring when expressing finer side of nature.

COMPOUND NUMBER: 15

Represents the individual operating in an environment of communications, freedom, action and movement. Considered a number of youthfulness. Success in developing original ideas enhanced. Magnet for financial and material success. "Focal point" for those in need of help or counseling.

* See Chapter 2

Section 2
BIRTHNAME VOWELS*
Heart's Desire
(Emotional Perspective)

BIRTHNAME: W I L L I A M   P H I L L I P   M I K E
(Vowels Underlined)

ALPHABET/NUMBERS: 1   11   1   1   1   5

                    3 plus 2 plus 6 equals 11

VOWEL NUMBER: 11

This is a *Master* number and is both intuitional and inspirational. Desire to reveal the vision of beauty available to all. Psychic ability inborn; counselor and "seer." Inventive with an electrical type of mind. Urge to be in the public limelight passing on "truth." Dreamer and visionary; do not love ideals more than people. Super Diplomat and Peacemaker, if "human" understanding is cultivated. Great interior strength; can carry great responsibility.

* See Chapter 3

Section 3
BIRTHNAME CONSONANTS*
Personality, As Others See Us
(Physical Perspective)

BIRTHNAME: W I L L I A M P H I L L I P M I K E
(Consonants Underlined)

ALPHABET/NUMBERS: 6   3 3   4 8 5 3 3 8 4   2

                 1 6   2 7   6

               7 plus 9 plus 6 equals 22

CONSONANT NUMBER: 22

You will be seen as either a "know-it-all" or an expert. Seen by many as being extremely practical, with your feet planted firmly on the ground. Even when broke, an appearance of wealth is projected. Many believe that you can make dreams come true.

* See Chapter 4

Section 4
BIRTHDATE*
Destiny, Life Path, Reality Cycle
(Intellectual Perspective)

BIRTHDATE: September 21, 1938

             9   3   21

         9 plus 3 plus 3 equals 15

        1 plus 5 equals 6

BIRTHDATE NUMBER: 6

Cycle of responsibility and balance, adjustment, understanding. To keep the scales of justice in balance. Parent, teacher of high ideals, and counselor. Service in the home and the community. Cornerstones are love, truth, beauty, and harmony. Innate ability of artistic expression and appreciation.

COMPOUND NUMBER: 15

The same as the Compound Number of the Full Name at Birth in Section 1 of the Numero-Log.

Section 5
PINNACLES*
Opportunities/Open Doors

FIRST PINNACLE: 3   (30 years—1968)
Develop creative and artistic ability. Imagination and feelings are on top; use them. Opportunities for writing, speaking, interior design, and stage/movie entertainment. Channel creative energies for greatest success.

SECOND PINNACLE: 6   (9 years to 1977)
Home duties and responsibilities are emphasized. Cultivate love and willing service. Money is made through much work and settling down. Happiness comes from giving and helping others (not a pinnacle for personal interests only). Pinnacle of Marriage—if you do, it will be a good one.

THIRD PINNACLE: 9   (9 years to 1986)
Highly charged and emotional period which could be difficult; learn to be impersonal and universal. Develop love, compassion, tolerance and service to others; inner response—sympathy and selflessness.

FOURTH PINNACLE: 3   (1987 for rest of life)
Same as First Pinnacle—except that I'm wiser now.

* See Chapter 7 Illustration for calculations.

Section 6
CHALLENGES*
Doors to be Opened

MAIN CHALLENGE: 6   (throughout life)
Be aware not to be overly idealistic, or risk becoming opinionated and self righteous. Learn to respect, not just tolerate, the views of others for true companionship and love; adjust to the fact that everyone is entitled to their point of view. Don't expect or try to make everyone adjust or cohform to "your" rules or way of thinking; you will be resented.
FIRST SUB-CHALLENGE: 6   (birth until 30—1968)
Same as the Main Challenge—this emphasizes the fact that the language of the Main Challenge is to be understood and acted upon for real success.
SECOND SUB-CHALLENGE: 0   (lasts 27 years to 1995)
The "zero" challenge is known as the challenge of CHOICE: you must choose for yourself and not rely on others to choose for you; know where your pitfalls lie. Includes the knowledge and talents of all the numbers. You know which way to turn, but you must *know* that you know, and then—CHOOSE.
FINAL SUB-CHALLENGE: 6   (remainder of life)
Same as the Main Challenge—again *emphasizes* the need to meet this challenge for greatest achievement.

* See Chapter 8 Illustration for calculations.

Section 7
GOAL POWER NUMBER*Final Opportunities

PURPOSE NUMBER: 6   (from Section 1 of the Numero-Log or Chapter 2)
(intuition)

  plus

DESTINY NUMBER: 6   (from Section 4 of the Numero-Log or Chapter 5)
(intellect)

  equals   ___
          12

GOAL POWER: 3   (influence in effect from mid-30's on)

Self expression is the keynote of this Goal Power vibration—in speaking, writing, or acting. Public Speaker, entertainer, publisher, or movie director are fertile areas for success and fulfillment. A naturalness with words, an excellent imagination and a good sense of humor are provided by this vibration. Don't scatter; concentrate on a few "select" goals.

COMPOUND NUMBER: 12
Indicates moral and ethical overtones.
The power of the #12 is directed toward achieving "at-one-ment." Favorable environment for reasoning and intellect, debates and speaking engagements.

* See Chapter 6

Section 8
PERSONAL YEARS*

BIRTHDAY: September 21 (9-21)

PERSONAL YEAR

1980 equals 3 (9 plus 21 plus 1980   equals 21   equals 3)
This year begins on the 21st of September 1979.
The #3 year is known as the cycle of fruition or success; it can be a "lucky" year if your efforts are not scattered and your energies are concentrated on priority goals. This can be a good selling period to market whatever you put into words. Popularity with friends, large groups and in the public. "Self expression" is the keynote in both the spoken and written word; take care and diligence in what you say, write and sign; read the fine print and be sure of what you read.

1981 equals 4 and begins on September 21, 1980.
The #4 year is a building year with detailed plans and a good "Framework" for future action. Make proper "connections," put your nose to the grindstone, and save. Don't let the feeling of restriction keep you from being creative; consolidate and retrench, for soon you will be quite active; expansion will be slow, but positive. This is a good cycle for firm friendships and balance in family relationships.

* See Chapter 9

Section 9
MONTHLY CYCLES
(Your Personal Year plus the Calendar Month)

For 1980, the Personal Year number is 3 (See Section 8). (The first month of the "year" is October 1979, which is a number 1 calendar month. Therefore, the *personal month* number for October 1979 is 3 plus 1 or 4.)

October 1979: 4
A building cycle; sacrifice now for future benefits; cycle of "*busy*ness"; pay attention to details. Key words are discipline and determination. Develop and express tolerance, mercy and sympathy.

November 1979: 5
A period of change, travel and movement. Varied situations, associations and acquaintances. Religious and spiritual work signified. Excellent for speaking, writing, selling and promoting self. Be aware of haste or speed in your decisions.

December 1979: 6
Symbolizes the law of balance and responsibility. Good earning period (and sharing). Good period for study projects and gaining knowledge.

January 1980: 4 (See information given for October 1979)

February 1980: 5 (See information given for November 1979)

March 1980: 6 (See information given for December 1979)

April 1980: 7
Good period for intellectual pursuits; pleasures of the mind. Pursue studies of a mystical nature. Put ideas into form; carry out plans where personal contact is unnecessary. Be punctual; don't allow delays to cause disappointment. Good period to contact your "center," but not to withdraw.

May 1980: 8
Force, energy and power are at your command. Avail yourself of what is at hand. Take the reins of your action and set your own direction. Power has been entrusted to you—use discretion.

June 1980: 9
Period for completing things signified by growth and gain. Cast off attitudes no longer valid; make way for the new. Emphasizes service to humanitarian associations. Cycle for eliminating negative influences.

July 1980: 1
New beginnings, new projects, new associates emphasized. Favorable for associations and/or work with men. Beneficial for expressing ambitions and making progress.

August 1980: 11
Visions, revelations, psychic illumination emphasized. Keynoted by

* See Chapter 9

metaphysics, philosophy and religion. Opportunity for "limelight" events and promoting ideas.

September 1980: 3
   Social popularity emphasized. Good period of a happy, positive outlook. Concentrate talents and energy for greatest success.

Section 10
SOUL QUALITIES DEVELOPMENT*

BIRTHNAME: W I L L I A M   P H I L L I P   M I K E

                   6 1 3 3 1 1 4   8 5 1 3 3 1 8   4 1 2 5

#1's	equal	6		#5's	equal	2
#2's	equal	1		#6's	equal	1
#3's	equal	4		#7's	equal	0**
#4's	equal	2		#8's	equal	2

** This is the area where work needs to be done.

SOUL QUALITY DEVELOPMENT: 7
   Avoided inner or spiritual development. Must learn the difference between illusion and reality. A prior decided unwillingness to train your mind in a logical and scientific manner. Must examine causes before coming to conclusions or accepting results. Develop "faith" as a replacement for trust in things and reliance on people.

* See Chapter 11

Section 11
COMPATIBILITY*
Personal Connections

THE ASPECT	THE ATTRACTION	THE NUMBERS OF	
		A	B
Purpose, Mission	Intuitive Spiritual	9	6
Heart's Desire	Emotional Psychological	6	11/2
Personality	Physical Personal	3	22/4
Destiny, Life Path	Intellectual Mental	8	6

PURPOSE: See Chapter 2 for the Language of these Numbers.
   Chart A's is 9. Chart B's is 6.
HEART'S DESIRE: See Chapter 3 for the Language of these Numbers.
   Chart A's is 6. Chart B's is 11 (also see #2).

PERSONALITY: See Chapter 4 for the Language of these Numbers.
Chart A's is 3. Chart B's is 22 (also see #4).
DESTINY: See Chapter 5 for the Language of these Numbers.
Chart A's is 8. Chart B's is 6.

Section 12
MISCELLANEOUS*

Names, Addresses, Licenses, Cities

NAMES: Use this section to plan and figure any names which you may want to consider in a possible change. Be sure to compare it to the language of the numbers of your birthname.

ADDRESSES: To be used if you wish to check out the vibrations of particular addresses with your vibrations.

LICENSES: This area can include anything from license plate numbers to contractor's license numbers to business license numbers, etc.

License Plate #: *878ACE* — 8 plus 7 plus 8 equals 23 or 5. **
Driver's License #: *M0895107* — The sum of this is 30 or 3. **

* See Chapter 13

** Read Chapters 2, 3, and 4 for the definitions of these numbers; then read Chapter 10 for the Compound Numbers.

CITIES: If you plan to move to another city, or are transferred to another city for your job, you can get an idea of how you will react to the new environment.

	Los Angeles	San Francisco	Phoenix
Total Name:	11	15/ 6	36/ 9
Vowels:	9	5	4
Consonants:	11	1	5

Appendix A
LIFE SPAN

PURPOSE: 6   (Section 1 of the Numero-Log)
To follow and teach the Golden Rule; Cosmic Parent. Music and theater arts are natural. To bring harmony and beauty to every environment.

VOWELS: 11   (Section 2 of the Numero-Log)
Master number of intuition and inspiration. Psychic ability inborn; counselor and "seer." Dreamer, Visionary; Super Diplomat, Peacemaker.

CONSONANTS: 22   (Section 3 of the Numero-Log)
Seen as either a "know-it-all" or an expert. Seen as extremely practical, with firm foundation. Even when broke, you project an appearance of wealth.

DESTINY: 6   (Section 4 of the Numero-Log)
Cornerstones are love, truth, beauty and harmony. To keep the scales of justice in balance. Parent, teacher of high ideals, counselor.

MAIN CHALLENGE: 6 (Section 6 of the Numero-Log)
Be aware of being overly opinionated and self righteous. Learn to respect the views of others. Don't expect everyone to conform to your rules.

Appendix B
MAJOR CYCLES

CURRENT PINNACLE: 9 (from 1978 to 1986)
A highly charged and emotional period. Learn to be impersonal (but not indifferent) and universal. Develop compassion, tolerance and service to others. Inner response—love, sympathy and selflessness.

CURRENT SUB-CHALLENGE: 0 (from 1969 to 1995)
The "zero" challenge is known as the challenge of CHOICE. You must choose for yourself and not rely on others to choose for you; know where your pitfalls lie. Includes the knowledge and talents of all the numbers. You know which way to turn, but you must *know* that you know, and then—CHOOSE.

GOAL POWER: 3 (1977 for rest of life)
Self expression is keynoted—in speaking, writing and acting. Public speaker, entertainer, publisher or movie director. Provides an excellent imagination, a good sense of humor, and a naturalness with words. Concentrate your energy and effort on a few "select" goals; don't scatter yourself.

15
Spiritual Masters
Moses, Buddha, Krishna, Christ

Although the personalities discussed in this chapter were spiritual masters, avatars, teachers and religious leaders, they were, at the same time, human beings experiencing physical reality. They may have been "divine by nature," but they were indeed also feeling, thinking, living and moving beings.

Each of these masters were serving a purpose and completing a mission in earthly form; each were seen a certain way by those around them; and each preferred a particular setting in which to experience this reality. Their lives unfolded within this "chosen" framework. And, like those who came before and after them, they had a blueprint from which radiated the vibrational patterns of their experiences.

In this chapter, I will reveal the language of the Birthname Numbers of Moses, Buddha and Krishna, as well as the Birthname *and* Birthdate of Jesus Christ, not because I can claim its validity through historical proof, but because of the very interesting and *revealing* analysis of the language behind that particular Birthdate Number.

Remember the science and language of numbers was known to exist *at least 11,000 years ago,* long before any of these spiritual masters lived on this earth. The language of their numbers was *not* defined by their lives, rather the blueprint for their life was defined by the language of their numbers.

MOSES

Vowels:	7		5		= 12	=	3
	M	O	S	E	S		
Consonants:	4	3		3	= 10	=	1
Total Name Number:					22		

PURPOSE (Name Number): = 22

This is a *Master* Number which represents the Super Statesman as well as the Master Builder. It symbolizes the building of roads and the laying of foundations which others will follow.

EMOTIONAL PERSPECTIVE (Vowels): = 3
Inherent in the #3 is the desire to express "self." It is an outgoing, dramatic and public vibration. It represents the "integration" of mind, body and soul.

PERSONALITY (Consonants): = 1
This reflects an aura of courage, daring, independence and leadership. It is seen as dominant and forceful.

BUDDHA

Vowels:		6			1	= 7	=	7
	B	U	D	D	H	A		
Consonants:	2	4	4	5		= 15	=	6
Total Name Number:						= 22		

PURPOSE (Name Number): = 22

This is a *Master* Number and presents the same blueprint as that of *Moses*. (NOTE: Differences can be seen in the nature of their emotional and physical perspective.)

EMOTIONAL PERSPECTIVE (Vowels) = 7
The patterns which flow from the number 7 reflect introspection, philosophy, and spirituality. The desire to reveal the nature of reality is inherent in the 7, as well as the ability to inspire. The number 7 is reserved, conservative and withdrawn.

PERSONALITY (Consonants) = 6
The number 6 enjoys the "quest" of meditation and contemplation and is seen as harmonious, calm and sympathetic. The number 6 is sought by others for advice and comfort.

KRISHNA

Vowels:			1		1	=	2	=	2
	K	R	I	S	H	N	A		
Consonants:	2 2		3	5	5		= 17	=	8
Total Name Number:							=	19	

PURPOSE (Name Number): = 19/ 1

The number 19 is the "most blessed" of all numbers. It represents the Alpha (#1) and the Omega (#9), and has within it the attributes of all the numbers. The number 1 symbolizes originality, independence, free will, self reliance, courage, initiative and leadership.

EMOTIONAL PERSPECTIVE (Vowels) = 2

The number 2 is the natural arbiter and peacemaker. It represents cooperation, kindness and sensitivity. It is nonaggaressive, and symbolizes association and parternships.

PERSONALITY (Consonants) = 8

Power and authority are reflected in the patterns of the number 8, as well as efficiency. Material and/or business problems are easily brought under control.

JESUS CHRIST

Vowels:		5	6			1		= 12	=	3
	J	E	S	U	S	C	H R I S T			
Consonants:	1	3	3	3	5 2	3 4	= 24	=	6	
Total Name Number:							= 36	=	9	

BIRTHDATE:	12	−	25	−	1			
Destiny:	3	+	7	+	1		= 11	
First Pinnacle:	3	+	7				= 10	= 1
Main Challenge:							= 2	
First Sub-Challenge:							= 4	

PURPOSE (Name Number): = 9

Bywords of the number 9 are compassion, tolerance, understanding and service. The number 9 represents spiritual leaders, teachers and healers, as well as humanitarians. It is the number of completion, impersonality and objectivity.

EMOTIONAL PERSPECTIVE (Vowels):   =   3
Same motivation as shown in the vowels of *Moses*.

PERSONALITY (Consonants):   =   6
Same description as that of *Buddha*.

DESTINY (Birthdate Number):   =   11
This is the *Master* Number of "Illumination." It is the number of inner guidance and faith. Psychic and intuitive power is inherent. The number 11 inspires by example and represents "The Peacemaker."

FIRST PINNACLE: =   1
This pinnacle is *34 years long* and starts at birth. The number 1 emphasizes individualization, creativity and independence. (NOTE; The Old Testament (Moses) symbolizes Universal Law, while the New Testament (Christ) symbolizes that law individualized.) This is the cycle of new beginnings, action and change. Christ was crucified in his *34th* year, the *last* year of his First Pinnacle.

MAIN CHALLENGE: =   2
This is the challenge of *"self* confidence." Emotional sensitivity and psychic power are inherent. The courage to speak the truth must be developed.

FIRST SUB-CHALLENGE: =   4
The first sub-challenge has the same duration as the first pinnacle, *34 years*. The number 4 is the number of the "Carpenter." It represents the square, hard work, discipline, perseverance and order.

(NOTE: The "coincidences" shown in the connections between the experiences of Jesus Christ and the patterns reflected in the language of the birthdate of 12 − 25 − 1, seem to almost *confirm* the validity of Christmas Day as the correct day of birth for Christ, regardless of the lack of written evidence or records.)

Additional understanding and meaning of the language of the numbers of these spiritual masters described in this chapter can be found in the meaning of the Compound Numbers in Chapter 10.

16
Beyond Numerology
Vibrational Interpretive Analysis
(V I A)

I believe that "everything under the sun is new" and that each and every day is a completely new experience. If, for instance, you were to develop your Numero-Log (Chapter 14) to include a description of each day of your experience, do not be surprised to find that the language of that day's vibrational pattern reveals a distinctly new "environment" which is indeed "different" from yesterday and from any "future" days.

And although each day may "seem" to be virtually the same (after all, most of the unfolding patterns remain consistent for certain periods), the day is, in fact, revealing new patterns and environments for you to experience. You, in essence, can "see" the patterns of each day by looking at the language of the numbers behind the day. You get an overview of the plan for that particular day—as it relates to your particular blueprint of experiences.

I do not recommend that you make a detailed layout of all of the days ahead of you, for, if you did, it would take all of the spontaneous responses which add spice to living, and make them "predictable." The understanding of the unfolding patterns in your experiencing should only provide you with a means of becoming more aware of the potential that exists in each day. So, if you feel the *need* to "examine" that potential for an important event which may be in the offing, that avenue will be available to you for your use.

If you really wanted to, you could write the story of your life from the numbers of your name and birthdate. You could develop volumes, then sections within each volume, then chapters within each section, and finally describe the scenes within each chapter. These scenes can be compared to the experiences which occur in each day of your life as new and different events.

This concept of being able to "define" each day is what gives rise to the premise that "everything under the sun is new," the opposite of contemporary and traditional thought that "nothing is new under the sun." Although most of the things you may see will be familiar and appear to be the same—the streets you drive down, the house you live in, the office you work at, the store where you shop—in reality, the opportunity for new experiences or rather the *potential* for new events and situations will be awaiting you. This "newness" is part of our experiencing as soon as we become aware of the day—as soon as we *awaken* to each day.

In the moment that you open your eyes and respond with the perception of all your senses, you have created a new pattern of experiencing in that environment. That day is the only conscious, perceptive experiencing of which you are aware (at least in this physical environment into which you were born) and is its own creation, its own pattern, its own universe of experiencing in and of itself. The phrase that says "We live each day only once" is not far from the truth. We miss a universe of experiences by worrying about what happened yesterday and what might happen tomorrow.

In looking at the language of numbers, our greatest reward comes from the understanding we derive from the interpretation of each number's vibrational patterns. In developing a technique to help to begin the process of interpretation, I discovered a concept which I call Vibrational Interpretive Analysis (the VIA process). However, VIA is more of a concept than a technique or application. It is something of which I can say "what it is" more than how to use it. However, from the understanding of what VIA is, and, of course, the desire to understand the language of your numbers, an understanding of the process of Vibrational Interpretive Analysis will follow.

Many times you walk into a room full of people and feel uncomfortable or something seems strange, or is amiss and you can't put your finger on it. Instead of reacting by deciding that you are going to have a terrible time, or that the person you just met is not desirable as a friend, or that you want to leave because you don't feel right, stop for a brief moment and get in tune with the environment. Try to pinpoint the "vibration" which is causing you the discomfort. Hopefully, once you understand what has caused your reaction, you can resolve the difference and proceed to enjoy the environment which you are experiencing.

This "getting in tune with" is part of the process of Vibrational Interpretive Analysis and helps you get "practice" in using your intuitive ability. VIA combines the technical knowledge of Numerology (the science of numbers), with the definition of the numerical vibrations (the language of numbers), with our innate ability to "see" (intuition) things that are part of what is happening (to see through the illusion or behind the appearance). Learn to respond more openly to the environment in which you find yourself, and to others and to potential events, rather than a specific individual reaction to the environment. Learn to understand the patterns of life's action, rather than reacting to a single event or a single person.

As you broaden your perspective on life and living, your ability to interpret the vibrations moving around you increases and comes with greater ease. Your experiencing is constantly changing and you cannot allow yourself to get caught in a framework of living which limits your participation and restricts your creative expression. Unless, that is, you *want* your life to be limited.

VIA analyzes the language of numbers through an interpretive process which looks at the interrelationship of all the numbers and their vibrational patterns. With VIA you can glance at all the aspects of a chart and find an "extra" facet pop up as a result of something within each of the vibrational patterns that come together. The realization comes through the interrelationship of the vibrational patterns and the natural working together of certain of the "facets" of each number. It's a matter of "seeing" the numbers and letting their sounds flow together so that more comes from the chart than just what the individual numbers say.

The greatest success comes from allowing your intuitive or psychic abilities to function within the framework of your analysis. You learn to develop that knack to "feel" where a person belongs as soon as you pick up the person's chart and make your first pass, without analyzing anything in the true sense of analysis. Then you go into the different areas of the chart to see additional information which can be gleaned from the basic patterns shown.

Vibrational Interpretive Analysis is the definition of my view of Numerology. We analyze the vibrational patterns of the number as defined by its language. The key to the analysis is within the definition of the number. You look at the language of the number in relation to the action, events and situations which are occurring around you.

The next step of VIA is interpretation which is divided into three parts. This includes interpretation of the analysis in relationship to (a) the different aspects of each number (Purpose, Destiny, etc.), (b) the same aspect of different numbers, and (c) different aspects of different numbers (i.e., in determining compatibility).

First there is the interpretation of *different aspects of the same number*. For instance, the number 8 has the number 8 Purpose, the number 8 Heart's Desire, and number 8 Personality, the number 8 Destiny, etc. If the number 8 vibrational pattern (or any number's pattern) shows up more than once in the blueprint, it is an indication of a certain additional degree of dominance by that number's vibratory force.

Understand that each separate aspect of the number presents a slightly different approach in defining a particular environment, even though the basis of the definition draws from the same root. Also important is your ability to relate the different aspects to what is happening in your life and their effect on the unfolding events. For as a specific number appears more frequently within a particular chart, the larger is the handwriting on the wall as to the direction in which you must move, inevitably—or be moved.

The next part of the interpretive phase of VIA is looking at the *same aspect of different numbers*. Always remember that VIA is the logical breaking down of those alternatives at which we can look, plus the application of our intuitive sense of knowing which alternatives are moving in the right direction. This part of the interpretive phase is most frequently used in the comparative analysis (compatibility) of the aspects of two different people or one person with the aspects of a business which they are about to start. It brings the relationship of the Mission/Purpose/Intuitive perspective of one number into focus as it interacts with the same aspect of another number.

As you look at the different relationships between people or between people, places or things, you look for the likeness and any potential "seeming" conflicts. There may be a misunderstanding between the people concerned or by the person concerned with his business as a result of certain vibrational patterns which may "feel" uncomfortable or hostile.

For instance, when comparing the number 8 Mission of one person with the number 3 Mission of another, part of the interpretation is to look at that relationship. Where are the likenesses? Where are the differences? How strong are the differences? Are they strong enough to cause any misunderstandings?

The interaction of the number 8 and the number 3 generally causes some friction, since the vibrational pattern of the number 8 which is the number of power, energy, authority and intuition (*feminine* aspect) seems to be in competition with the vibrational pattern of the number 3 which is the number of ambition, self expression, public action and intuition (*masculine* aspect).

For some evasive reason, most numerological explanations of these numbers say only that the number 8 and the number 3 should avoid each other since they do not "get along." Instead the explanation *should be* that you *do not* have to avoid the "conflict." You should understand what impinging vibrational pattern is unfolding so that you can interrelate and experience the unfolding events to your benefit and learning. As you understand the language of a person's vibrational pattern, the conflict begins to dissolve. You learn how to "speak" the language of everyone with whom you interact, instead of reacting to an unknown and predominantly groundless fear.

The third part of the interpretive phase of VIA considers the *different aspects of different numbers*. It takes a look at the variables which enter into a relationship as a result of a substantive difference in aspect orientation. You may have a number 8 Mission off of your name and a number 3 Destiny off of your birthdate. Again, interpretation always involves relationships between numbers and their vibrations. What you do when looking at this part of the interpretive process is to ask yourself the question, "What does that mean to me relative to my experiencing and action?"

One of the first things to do is to add the number of the Mission to the number of Destiny in order to find your Goal Power Number, which is part of the interpretation. Simply stated, you combine what you know with your innate ablity to think about things and reach conclusions, and your capacity to feel things emotionally (for you know that when you feel strongly about anything it will affect your interpretation—and therefore your conclusions).

For instance, when you walk into a room and the atmosphere feels "high" what you are experiencing is the predominance of the "best" (or highest aspect) vibrational outflow of the people in the room, no matter what their "individual" vibration. Normally, a room full of people is the interrelated expression of different aspects of different numbers. If you walk into a room full of "gloom" then you should become alerted to the fact that there is a great deal of misunderstanding, distortion and "protective" reaction occurring within the atmosphere—and act accordingly.

If the room is "high," it uplifts anyone coming in; if the room is "low," it will tend to bring a person "down" to its level unless the person is aware of the interacting patterns. Therefore part of the interpretation is the *translation* of the interacting "moods" that flow from the vibrational patterns of the people with whom you are experiencing and the events and circumstances which are unfolding within those patterns.

Even when a psychic "reads" you, it involves a "translation" or interpretation of pictures, symbols, "feelings" into a language which the person being "read" can understand and use. At least when you are working with a person's "numbers," you have a basis of language from which to begin the interpretation. You have a reference point, a pattern on which you can focus and from which you can draw unfolding (potential) events.

My prime motivation in my approach is the desire to help people reach a clearer recognition of themselves and their life experiences through understanding the language of their numbers. I wish to introduce people to the concept of keeping in tune with their own blueprint while improving on it until their house is built to their specifications. And, I want to show people a painless, relatively easy way of getting in touch with themselves without the need of psychiatrists or counselors or organizations who promise great success if you use their techniques. I hope this can free them to develop "faith" in themselves and not be bound by the belief systems of others.

When you acknowledge the fact that you are *already* aware, then you only need to express that awareness in an ever-expanding environment.
You can experience your own being by starting where you are now, and experiencing the excitement of being both a participant and an observer of the life unfolding in front of you.

17

"The Whole is Greater Than the Sum of Its Parts"

Beyond the Language of Numbers

The proper use of Numerology along with an understanding of the language of numbers allows a person to become aware of the particular perspective that each day brings to their experience. You can align yourself with the "flow" of the day's events. This allows you to prepare yourself for each new set of experiences, but not by maintaining yesterday's perspective (for that has passed) nor by trying to "guess" what tomorrow's should be. You can learn to "feel" what is unfolding today. The "feel" you get comes from the sense of being in tune with and resonating to the day's vibrational patterns.

The sense of resonance is the final and most important aspect of the process of Vibrational Interpretive Analysis (VIA) and places the emphasis on our use of the faculty of intuition. For it is your intuition which brings VIA's most successful results. The language of numbers gives you that reference or "focal" point toward which your intuition can be directed and from which you can proceed to interpret with surprising accuracy and meaning. You are then able to center your direction and focus in on the appropriate unfolding environment for you.

Numerolinguistics is the name of the approach I take in developing and explaining the connection between each person's "numbers" and certain vibrational patterns which define a particular environment. Numerolinguistics, the study of the nature and scope of the language of numbers, places the emphasis on the *language* of numbers and not the science. The importance is in translating and properly interpreting those numbers that this science has given you.

Anyone can pick up a Numerology book, figure out their Destiny Number and then turn the page for the definition. That is a very simple level of understanding and interpreting your numbers. But, more important than the numbers, is the interpretation and the understanding of the language *behind* the numbers which shows you the vibrational patterns and their interrelationships as they are unfolding.

"The whole is greater than the sum of its parts" is a familiar statement to most of us. We understand that the parts taken by themselves are isolated; they produce a greater benefit by working as a "team." Traditionally, Numerology would show people how to determine their individual numbers, or parts, then let it go at that. Understanding the language behind numbers shows how these various parts work together and how they can be applied to real life events and circumstances.

I have developed Numerolinguistics and Vibrational Interpretive Analysis for the express purpose of helping people to use the "numbers of their life's pattern" as a basis for awareness and understanding of their life experiences. They can give one that blueprint or pattern upon which one can build a strong, beautiful and loving "home."

The language of the numbers can tell you where you are and then point you in the right direction. You do not have to worry any longer about what has gone past, because it has passed; it's only important to understand these past experiences in light of the present and the future vibrational patterns you are experiencing so that you will be in better "resonance" and more "in tune" with your life *as it unfolds* before you.

Numerolinguistics can also lead you to the understanding of the very real purpose which each one of us has. You will no longer have to ask yourself the question, "What should I be doing with my life?" You can now perceive the type of environments in which you will be able to achieve the greatest satisfaction and fulfillment. You will be able to see more clearly the direction in which you need to proceed to achieve just that satisfaction. By discovering the "special" language of your numbers, you will find yourself more eagerly anticipating each day and each new life experience as it presents itself.

The further you develop your understanding of Numerolinguistics and VIA, the more you will discover that your intuitive ability is functioning at a greater frequency. You will soon find that you can rely on your *intuition* in making decisions because you have begun to automatically, and probably unconsciously, apply what I call "intuitive logic." Intuitive logic combines the use of sense perception, your abilty to think and to draw conclusions, with that sense of "direct knowing" that comes from your intuitive faculties.

You begin to be more "in tune" with all of the aspects of your being which are part and parcel of your life's environment. Intuition takes over and begins to function normally as you start to have "faith" in its "correctness." And the more your intuition is working for you, the greater your ability to interpret the numbers of others. In fact, you'll probably be amazed at the discoveries you will make about others and the rapport that will flow between you. Our greatest understanding has always come from the direct flowing of our intuition. For it is our intuitive sense that guides us to the proper selection of a goal, event, circumstance or person out of the multitude of choices which confronts us every day.

This "new" perception of things will help you become more and more aware of the number of things which are occurring within your patterns of experiencing and the patterns of others with whom you come in contact. Both your inner and outer perception will increase and expand and this "sharpened awareness" will allow you to strengthen the bond between you and the people and events around you.

As you sharpen your inner and outer vision, you begin not only to strengthen existing relationships, but also increase the number of your relationships. You will attract to you certain kinds of relationships and people for your own experiencing and expansion.

Clearly your viewpoint will also expand and you will discover that you are really a plural individual. This means that you have the innate ability to assume a variety of different roles, effectively and successfully. You will then discover that these roles are all you, and all of them are real, and that each of these "whole parts" are contributing to the greater part, which is the *bigger and better* (i.e. more productive and more fulfilled) YOU.

For example, you can be a successful judge on the bench, and also be a successful teacher of banking and finance with no seeming connection between the two roles. And, at the same time, you could play an incredibly beautiful piano because of your Soul's Urge which is encouraging you to express yourself.

This expansion of viewpoint means that as your perception broadens, as you express that awareness which you already have (we are well beyond the need to learn self-awareness, and have always been so), and as you permit yourself to envision greater things, you would be completely surprised at the increased activity and experiences in which you found yourself participating.

Yes, we are plural individuals. We are teachers, advisors, editors, musicians and accountants, and all at the same time, only not necessarily expressing each aspect at the same time. We are many people expressing differently for different people. After all, we do live in a changing environment which constantly demands our attention. We are our Mission, our Purpose, our Challenges, our Opportunities, our Heart's Desire and our Personality. We are what we think, what we feel, what we wear, what we eat, where we work and what we learn. And we are more.

There are many things to be gleaned from the language of numbers, a great deal of knowledge to be had for the taking. The kind of knowledge that I am talking about is based on the premise that says "the map is not the territory." That premise is taken from the book *The World of Null-A* by A. E. Van Vogt. It is based on the concept of viewing things beyond the logic of Aristotle, the logic of philosophy and science, and beyond the use of common sense only. It is a concept of knowledge that says the map is only a map and may or may not be the territory to which we are going.

When you look at your blueprint, what you see is only a map of patterns. And you know that you have the capability, the talents and the power to shape those patterns so that as the territory changes and shifts, so will the map. Each time you look at the map (blueprint), it will be slightly different than the previous time, and will continue to change with each day that you experience. And it will automatically allow you to be aware of the multiplicity of choices which are available to you.

The process that flows from this concept of understanding numbers provides you with a framework for participation. Your creativity will be heightened by virtue of the fact that you are getting in touch with the many parts of you, some of which you may not previously have recognized. All of a sudden you discover latent talents beginning to open up!

We know that we have the potential within ourselves to be more creative and productive than we are. It isn't an entirely new viewpoint. It is an enlargement of a viewpoint that already exists, but is not being fully explained and utilized. I can provide a key that can unlock doors for you. But I cannot unlock your doors; only you can do that.

In this framework of participation, you are both the observer and the actor (participator). You set the stage, you act upon that stage, and you are the audience. The greatest advantage in seeing your blueprint is to know what you potentially are. You follow a similar process when you are dreaming. You watch the dream unfold as you participate in the action of the dream.

If you know that you are both the observer and participator at all times, you do not have to be "conscious" of that fact in order to benefit from that knowledge. You only have to know that it is happening. You only have to allow yourself to act and react to your environment, the people around you and action unfolding. Too many times people are just observers. They fail to fully participate in the action by "limiting" their involvement. Those who just jump in and become absorbed by the action, not taking time to observe and see the objectivity of things, miss the trees for the forest. However, we don't have to miss anything. All we have to do is to consciously set priorities for what we consider to be right for us.

The final aspect of this process of interpretation is that our real goal is to move beyond the language of numbers, Numerolinguistics, Vibrational Interpretive Analysis, and blueprint. You lay down your foundation, determine your direction and then take action, action that will move you forward in your experiencing. The past is no longer a basis for living and expressing. You can now begin to take steps that will lead you from awareness to participation. Once you *understand* the blueprint or pattern of your own experiences, you will rarely have to refer to it again.

You start where you are, with your birthname and birthdate. You move beyond the language of numbers to the language of your own experiencing. No matter how small a step you first take; once you get started in the direction of your pattern of living, you will continue to move in that direction. Eventually, you will achieve the fulfillment of living that you have been searching for. So, if anyone comments about what's in a birthdate or what's in a name, you will know that there is more than anyone would ever think possible.

Epilogue

The material in this book is not a technical treatise on Numerology or Numerolinguistics, nor was it intended to be. To clutter its pages with any more information would only confuse and complicate the nature of the subject. To go any further would be burdensome to anyone who wishes only to avail themselves of a basic understanding of the nature of their life's unfolding patterns.

I present a final word here about the "two" systems of Numerology. Whichever system you choose to use or advocate, you must make a commitment to that system. It must be "100%" for to "believe" in the validity of another is not only a contradiction in terms, but also destroys the credibility of the system you claim is valid.

Whatever you value, whatever you believe, whatever you use, remember this—in truth, we can really *do* whatever we choose and *be* whatever we want to be. All we have to do is *permit* ourselves to choose and to *allow* ourselves to be. It is our life, our experiencing, our reality, and we can attain a nearly complete fulfillment of being and its infinite potential, *if we choose.*

A Personal Word From Melvin Powers
Publisher, Wilshire Book Company

Dear Friend:

My goal is to publish interesting, informative, and inspirational books. You can help me accomplish this by answering the following questions, either by phone or by mail. Or, if convenient for you, I would welcome the opportunity to visit with you in my office and hear your comments in person.

Did you enjoy reading this book? Why?

Would you enjoy reading another similar book?

What idea in the book impressed you the most?

If applicable to your situation, have you incorporated this idea in your daily life?

Is there a chapter that could serve as a theme for an entire book? Please explain.

If you have an idea for a book, I would welcome discussing it with you. If you already have one in progress, write or call me concerning possible publication. I can be reached at (213) 875-1711 or (213) 983-1105.

Sincerely yours,
Melvin Powers

12015 Sherman Road
North Hollywood, California 91605

MELVIN POWERS SELF-IMPROVEMENT LIBRARY

ASTROLOGY

_____ ASTROLOGY: HOW TO CHART YOUR HOROSCOPE *Max Heindel*	3.00
_____ ASTROLOGY: YOUR PERSONAL SUN-SIGN GUIDE *Beatrice Ryder*	3.00
_____ ASTROLOGY FOR EVERYDAY LIVING *Janet Harris*	2.00
_____ ASTROLOGY MADE EASY *Astarte*	3.00
_____ ASTROLOGY MADE PRACTICAL *Alexandra Kayhle*	3.00
_____ ASTROLOGY, ROMANCE, YOU AND THE STARS *Anthony Norvell*	4.00
_____ MY WORLD OF ASTROLOGY *Sydney Omarr*	5.00
_____ THOUGHT DIAL *Sidney Omarr*	4.00
_____ WHAT THE STARS REVEAL ABOUT THE MEN IN YOUR LIFE *Thelma White*	3.00

BRIDGE

_____ BRIDGE BIDDING MADE EASY *Edwin B. Kantar*	7.00
_____ BRIDGE CONVENTIONS *Edwin B. Kantar*	7.00
_____ BRIDGE HUMOR *Edwin B. Kantar*	5.00
_____ COMPETITIVE BIDDING IN MODERN BRIDGE *Edgar Kaplan*	4.00
_____ DEFENSIVE BRIDGE PLAY COMPLETE *Edwin B. Kantar*	10.00
_____ GAMESMAN BRIDGE—Play Better with Kantar *Edwin B. Kantar*	5.00
_____ HOW TO IMPROVE YOUR BRIDGE *Alfred Sheinwold*	5.00
_____ IMPROVING YOUR BIDDING SKILLS *Edwin B. Kantar*	4.00
_____ INTRODUCTION TO DEFENDER'S PLAY *Edwin B. Kantar*	3.00
_____ KANTAR FOR THE DEFENSE *Edwin B. Kantar*	5.00
_____ SHORT CUT TO WINNING BRIDGE *Alfred Sheinwold*	3.00
_____ TEST YOUR BRIDGE PLAY *Edwin B. Kantar*	5.00
_____ VOLUME 2—TEST YOUR BRIDGE PLAY *Edwin B. Kantar*	5.00
_____ WINNING DECLARER PLAY *Dorothy Hayden Truscott*	4.00

BUSINESS, STUDY & REFERENCE

_____ CONVERSATION MADE EASY *Elliot Russell*	3.00
_____ EXAM SECRET *Dennis B. Jackson*	3.00
_____ FIX-IT BOOK *Arthur Symons*	2.00
_____ HOW TO DEVELOP A BETTER SPEAKING VOICE *M. Hellier*	3.00
_____ HOW TO MAKE A FORTUNE IN REAL ESTATE *Albert Winnikoff*	4.00
_____ INCREASE YOUR LEARNING POWER *Geoffrey A. Dudley*	3.00
_____ MAGIC OF NUMBERS *Robert Tocquet*	2.00
_____ PRACTICAL GUIDE TO BETTER CONCENTRATION *Melvin Powers*	3.00
_____ PRACTICAL GUIDE TO PUBLIC SPEAKING *Maurice Forley*	3.00
_____ 7 DAYS TO FASTER READING *William S. Schaill*	3.00
_____ SONGWRITERS' RHYMING DICTIONARY *Jane Shaw Whitfield*	5.00
_____ SPELLING MADE EASY *Lester D. Basch & Dr. Milton Finkelstein*	3.00
_____ STUDENT'S GUIDE TO BETTER GRADES *J. A. Rickard*	3.00
_____ TEST YOURSELF—Find Your Hidden Talent *Jack Shafer*	3.00
_____ YOUR WILL & WHAT TO DO ABOUT IT *Attorney Samuel G. Kling*	3.00

CALLIGRAPHY

_____ ADVANCED CALLIGRAPHY *Katherine Jeffares*	7.00
_____ CALLIGRAPHER'S REFERENCE BOOK *Anne Leptich & Jacque Evans*	7.00
_____ CALLIGRAPHY—The Art of Beautiful Writing *Katherine Jeffares*	7.00
_____ CALLIGRAPHY FOR FUN & PROFIT *Anne Leptich & Jacque Evans*	7.00
_____ CALLIGRAPHY MADE EASY *Tina Serafini*	7.00

CHESS & CHECKERS

_____ BEGINNER'S GUIDE TO WINNING CHESS *Fred Reinfeld*	4.00
_____ CHECKERS MADE EASY *Tom Wiswell*	2.00
_____ CHESS IN TEN EASY LESSONS *Larry Evans*	3.00
_____ CHESS MADE EASY *Milton L. Hanauer*	3.00
_____ CHESS PROBLEMS FOR BEGINNERS *edited by Fred Reinfeld*	2.00
_____ CHESS SECRETS REVEALED *Fred Reinfeld*	2.00
_____ CHESS STRATEGY—An Expert's Guide *Fred Reinfeld*	2.00
_____ CHESS TACTICS FOR BEGINNERS *edited by Fred Reinfeld*	3.00
_____ CHESS THEORY & PRACTICE *Morry & Mitchell*	2.00
_____ HOW TO WIN AT CHECKERS *Fred Reinfeld*	3.00
_____ 1001 BRILLIANT WAYS TO CHECKMATE *Fred Reinfeld*	4.00
_____ 1001 WINNING CHESS SACRIFICES & COMBINATIONS *Fred Reinfeld*	4.00
_____ SOVIET CHESS *Edited by R. G. Wade*	3.00

COOKERY & HERBS

_____ CULPEPER'S HERBAL REMEDIES *Dr. Nicholas Culpeper*	3.00
_____ FAST GOURMET COOKBOOK *Poppy Cannon*	2.50
_____ GINSENG The Myth & The Truth *Joseph P. Hou*	3.00
_____ HEALING POWER OF HERBS *May Bethel*	4.00
_____ HEALING POWER OF NATURAL FOODS *May Bethel*	3.00
_____ HERB HANDBOOK *Dawn MacLeod*	3.00
_____ HERBS FOR COOKING AND HEALING *Dr. Donald Law*	2.00
_____ HERBS FOR HEALTH—How to Grow & Use Them *Louise Evans Doole*	3.00
_____ HOME GARDEN COOKBOOK—Delicious Natural Food Recipes *Ken Kraft*	3.00
_____ MEDICAL HERBALIST *edited by Dr. J. R. Yemm*	3.00
_____ NATURAL FOOD COOKBOOK *Dr. Harry C. Bond*	3.00
_____ NATURE'S MEDICINES *Richard Lucas*	3.00
_____ VEGETABLE GARDENING FOR BEGINNERS *Hugh Wiberg*	2.00
_____ VEGETABLES FOR TODAY'S GARDENS *R. Milton Carleton*	2.00
_____ VEGETARIAN COOKERY *Janet Walker*	4.00
_____ VEGETARIAN COOKING MADE EASY & DELECTABLE *Veronica Vezza*	3.00
_____ VEGETARIAN DELIGHTS—A Happy Cookbook for Health *K. R. Mehta*	2.00
_____ VEGETARIAN GOURMET COOKBOOK *Joyce McKinnel*	3.00

GAMBLING & POKER

_____ ADVANCED POKER STRATEGY & WINNING PLAY *A. D. Livingston*	5.00
_____ HOW NOT TO LOSE AT POKER *Jeffrey Lloyd Castle*	3.00
_____ HOW TO WIN AT DICE GAMES *Skip Frey*	3.00
_____ HOW TO WIN AT POKER *Terence Reese & Anthony T. Watkins*	3.00
_____ SECRETS OF WINNING POKER *George S. Coffin*	3.00
_____ WINNING AT CRAPS *Dr. Lloyd T. Commins*	3.00
_____ WINNING AT GIN *Chester Wander & Cy Rice*	3.00
_____ WINNING AT POKER—An Expert's Guide *John Archer*	3.00
_____ WINNING AT 21—An Expert's Guide *John Archer*	5.00
_____ WINNING POKER SYSTEMS *Norman Zadeh*	3.00

HEALTH

_____ BEE POLLEN *Lynda Lyngheim & Jack Scagnetti*	3.00
_____ DR. LINDNER'S SPECIAL WEIGHT CONTROL METHOD *P. G. Lindner, M.D.*	1.50
_____ HELP YOURSELF TO BETTER SIGHT *Margaret Darst Corbett*	3.00
_____ HOW TO IMPROVE YOUR VISION *Dr. Robert A. Kraskin*	3.00
_____ HOW YOU CAN STOP SMOKING PERMANENTLY *Ernest Caldwell*	3.00
_____ MIND OVER PLATTER *Peter G. Lindner, M.D.*	3.00
_____ NATURE'S WAY TO NUTRITION & VIBRANT HEALTH *Robert J. Scrutton*	3.00
_____ NEW CARBOHYDRATE DIET COUNTER *Patti Lopez-Pereira*	1.50
_____ QUICK & EASY EXERCISES FOR FACIAL BEAUTY *Judy Smith-deal*	2.00
_____ QUICK & EASY EXERCISES FOR FIGURE BEAUTY *Judy Smith-deal*	2.00
_____ REFLEXOLOGY *Dr. Maybelle Segal*	3.00
_____ REFLEXOLOGY FOR GOOD HEALTH *Anna Kaye & Don C. Matchan*	3.00
_____ YOU CAN LEARN TO RELAX *Dr. Samuel Gutwirth*	3.00
_____ YOUR ALLERGY—What To Do About It *Allan Knight, M.D.*	3.00

HOBBIES

_____ BEACHCOMBING FOR BEGINNERS *Norman Hickin*	2.00
_____ BLACKSTONE'S MODERN CARD TRICKS *Harry Blackstone*	3.00
_____ BLACKSTONE'S SECRETS OF MAGIC *Harry Blackstone*	3.00
_____ COIN COLLECTING FOR BEGINNERS *Burton Hobson & Fred Reinfeld*	3.00
_____ ENTERTAINING WITH ESP *Tony 'Doc' Shiels*	2.00
_____ 400 FASCINATING MAGIC TRICKS YOU CAN DO *Howard Thurston*	4.00
_____ HOW I TURN JUNK INTO FUN AND PROFIT *Sari*	3.00
_____ HOW TO WRITE A HIT SONG & SELL IT *Tommy Boyce*	7.00
_____ JUGGLING MADE EASY *Rudolf Dittrich*	2.00
_____ MAGIC FOR ALL AGES *Walter Gibson*	4.00
_____ MAGIC MADE EASY *Byron Wels*	2.00
_____ STAMP COLLECTING FOR BEGINNERS *Burton Hobson*	3.00

HORSE PLAYERS' WINNING GUIDES

_____ BETTING HORSES TO WIN *Les Conklin*	3.00
_____ ELIMINATE THE LOSERS *Bob McKnight*	3.00
_____ HOW TO PICK WINNING HORSES *Bob McKnight*	3.00

____ HOW TO WIN AT THE RACES *Sam (The Genius) Lewin*	5.00
____ HOW YOU CAN BEAT THE RACES *Jack Kavanagh*	3.00
____ MAKING MONEY AT THE RACES *David Barr*	3.00
____ PAYDAY AT THE RACES *Les Conklin*	3.00
____ SMART HANDICAPPING MADE EASY *William Bauman*	3.00
____ SUCCESS AT THE HARNESS RACES *Barry Meadow*	3.00
____ WINNING AT THE HARNESS RACES—An Expert's Guide *Nick Cammarano*	3.00

HUMOR

____ HOW TO BE A COMEDIAN FOR FUN & PROFIT *King & Laufer*	2.00
____ HOW TO FLATTEN YOUR TUSH *Coach Marge Reardon*	2.00
____ HOW TO MAKE LOVE TO YOURSELF *Ron Stevens & Joy Grdnic*	3.00
____ JOKE TELLER'S HANDBOOK *Bob Orben*	3.00
____ JOKES FOR ALL OCCASIONS *Al Schock*	3.00
____ 2000 NEW LAUGHS FOR SPEAKERS *Bob Orben*	4.00
____ 2,500 JOKES TO START 'EM LAUGHING *Bob Orben*	3.00

HYPNOTISM

____ ADVANCED TECHNIQUES OF HYPNOSIS *Melvin Powers*	2.00
____ BRAINWASHING AND THE CULTS *Paul A. Verdier, Ph.D.*	3.00
____ CHILDBIRTH WITH HYPNOSIS *William S. Kroger, M.D.*	5.00
____ HOW TO SOLVE Your Sex Problems with Self-Hypnosis *Frank S. Caprio, M.D.*	5.00
____ HOW TO STOP SMOKING THRU SELF-HYPNOSIS *Leslie M. LeCron*	3.00
____ HOW TO USE AUTO-SUGGESTION EFFECTIVELY *John Duckworth*	3.00
____ HOW YOU CAN BOWL BETTER USING SELF-HYPNOSIS *Jack Heise*	3.00
____ HOW YOU CAN PLAY BETTER GOLF USING SELF-HYPNOSIS *Jack Heise*	3.00
____ HYPNOSIS AND SELF-HYPNOSIS *Bernard Hollander, M.D.*	3.00
____ HYPNOTISM *(Originally published in 1893)* *Carl Sextus*	5.00
____ HYPNOTISM & PSYCHIC PHENOMENA *Simeon Edmunds*	4.00
____ HYPNOTISM MADE EASY *Dr. Ralph Winn*	3.00
____ HYPNOTISM MADE PRACTICAL *Louis Orton*	3.00
____ HYPNOTISM REVEALED *Melvin Powers*	2.00
____ HYPNOTISM TODAY *Leslie LeCron and Jean Bordeaux, Ph.D.*	5.00
____ MODERN HYPNOSIS *Lesley Kuhn & Salvatore Russo, Ph.D.*	5.00
____ NEW CONCEPTS OF HYPNOSIS *Bernard C. Gindes, M.D.*	5.00
____ NEW SELF-HYPNOSIS *Paul Adams*	4.00
____ POST-HYPNOTIC INSTRUCTIONS—Suggestions for Therapy *Arnold Furst*	3.00
____ PRACTICAL GUIDE TO SELF-HYPNOSIS *Melvin Powers*	3.00
____ PRACTICAL HYPNOTISM *Philip Magonet, M.D.*	3.00
____ SECRETS OF HYPNOTISM *S. J. Van Pelt, M.D.*	5.00
____ SELF-HYPNOSIS A Conditioned-Response Technique *Laurence Sparks*	5.00
____ SELF-HYPNOSIS Its Theory, Technique & Application *Melvin Powers*	3.00
____ THERAPY THROUGH HYPNOSIS *edited by Raphael H. Rhodes*	4.00

JUDAICA

____ HOW TO LIVE A RICHER & FULLER LIFE *Rabbi Edgar F. Magnin*	2.00
____ MODERN ISRAEL *Lily Edelman*	2.00
____ SERVICE OF THE HEART *Evelyn Garfiel, Ph.D.*	4.00
____ STORY OF ISRAEL IN COINS *Jean & Maurice Gould*	2.00
____ STORY OF ISRAEL IN STAMPS *Maxim & Gabriel Shamir*	1.00
____ TONGUE OF THE PROPHETS *Robert St. John*	5.00

JUST FOR WOMEN

____ COSMOPOLITAN'S GUIDE TO MARVELOUS MEN Fwd. by *Helen Gurley Brown*	3.00
____ COSMOPOLITAN'S HANG-UP HANDBOOK Foreword by *Helen Gurley Brown*	4.00
____ COSMOPOLITAN'S LOVE BOOK—A Guide to Ecstasy in Bed	4.00
____ COSMOPOLITAN'S NEW ETIQUETTE GUIDE Fwd. by *Helen Gurley Brown*	4.00
____ I AM A COMPLEAT WOMAN *Doris Hagopian & Karen O'Connor Sweeney*	3.00
____ JUST FOR WOMEN—A Guide to the Female Body *Richard E. Sand, M.D.*	5.00
____ NEW APPROACHES TO SEX IN MARRIAGE *John E. Eichenlaub, M.D.*	3.00
____ SEXUALLY ADEQUATE FEMALE *Frank S. Caprio, M.D.*	3.00
____ YOUR FIRST YEAR OF MARRIAGE *Dr. Tom McGinnis*	3.00

MARRIAGE, SEX & PARENTHOOD

____ ABILITY TO LOVE *Dr. Allan Fromme*	5.00
____ ENCYCLOPEDIA OF MODERN SEX & LOVE TECHNIQUES *Macandrew*	5.00
____ GUIDE TO SUCCESSFUL MARRIAGE *Drs. Albert Ellis & Robert Harper*	5.00

_____ HOW TO RAISE AN EMOTIONALLY HEALTHY, HAPPY CHILD *A. Ellis*	4.00
_____ SEX WITHOUT GUILT *Albert Ellis, Ph.D.*	5.00
_____ SEXUALLY ADEQUATE MALE *Frank S. Caprio, M.D.*	3.00

MELVIN POWERS' MAIL ORDER LIBRARY

_____ HOW TO GET RICH IN MAIL ORDER *Melvin Powers*	10.00
_____ HOW TO WRITE A GOOD ADVERTISEMENT *Victor O. Schwab*	15.00
_____ MAIL ORDER MADE EASY *J. Frank Brumbaugh*	10.00
_____ U.S. MAIL ORDER SHOPPER'S GUIDE *Susan Spitzer*	10.00

METAPHYSICS & OCCULT

_____ BOOK OF TALISMANS, AMULETS & ZODIACAL GEMS *William Pavitt*	5.00
_____ CONCENTRATION—A Guide to Mental Mastery *Mouni Sadhu*	4.00
_____ CRITIQUES OF GOD *Edited by Peter Angeles*	7.00
_____ EXTRA-TERRESTRIAL INTELLIGENCE—The First Encounter	6.00
_____ FORTUNE TELLING WITH CARDS *P. Foli*	3.00
_____ HANDWRITING ANALYSIS MADE EASY *John Marley*	4.00
_____ HANDWRITING TELLS *Nadya Olyanova*	5.00
_____ HOW TO INTERPRET DREAMS, OMENS & FORTUNE TELLING SIGNS *Gettings*	3.00
_____ HOW TO UNDERSTAND YOUR DREAMS *Geoffrey A. Dudley*	3.00
_____ ILLUSTRATED YOGA *William Zorn*	3.00
_____ IN DAYS OF GREAT PEACE *Mouni Sadhu*	3.00
_____ LSD—THE AGE OF MIND *Bernard Roseman*	2.00
_____ MAGICIAN—His Training and Work *W. E. Butler*	3.00
_____ MEDITATION *Mouni Sadhu*	5.00
_____ MODERN NUMEROLOGY *Morris C. Goodman*	3.00
_____ NUMEROLOGY—ITS FACTS AND SECRETS *Ariel Yvon Taylor*	3.00
_____ NUMEROLOGY MADE EASY *W. Mykian*	3.00
_____ PALMISTRY MADE EASY *Fred Gettings*	3.00
_____ PALMISTRY MADE PRACTICAL *Elizabeth Daniels Squire*	4.00
_____ PALMISTRY SECRETS REVEALED *Henry Frith*	3.00
_____ PROPHECY IN OUR TIME *Martin Ebon*	2.50
_____ PSYCHOLOGY OF HANDWRITING *Nadya Olyanova*	5.00
_____ SUPERSTITION—Are You Superstitious? *Eric Maple*	2.00
_____ TAROT *Mouni Sadhu*	6.00
_____ TAROT OF THE BOHEMIANS *Papus*	5.00
_____ WAYS TO SELF-REALIZATION *Mouni Sadhu*	3.00
_____ WHAT YOUR HANDWRITING REVEALS *Albert E. Hughes*	3.00
_____ WITCHCRAFT, MAGIC & OCCULTISM—A Fascinating History *W. B. Crow*	5.00
_____ WITCHCRAFT—THE SIXTH SENSE *Justine Glass*	4.00
_____ WORLD OF PSYCHIC RESEARCH *Hereward Carrington*	2.00

SELF-HELP & INSPIRATIONAL

_____ DAILY POWER FOR JOYFUL LIVING *Dr. Donald Curtis*	5.00
_____ DYNAMIC THINKING *Melvin Powers*	2.00
_____ EXUBERANCE—Your Guide to Happiness & Fulfillment *Dr. Paul Kurtz*	3.00
_____ GREATEST POWER IN THE UNIVERSE *U. S. Andersen*	5.00
_____ GROW RICH WHILE YOU SLEEP *Ben Sweetland*	3.00
_____ GROWTH THROUGH REASON *Albert Ellis, Ph.D.*	4.00
_____ GUIDE TO DEVELOPING YOUR POTENTIAL *Herbert A. Otto, Ph.D.*	3.00
_____ GUIDE TO LIVING IN BALANCE *Frank S. Caprio, M.D.*	2.00
_____ GUIDE TO PERSONAL HAPPINESS *Albert Ellis, Ph.D. & Irving Becker, Ed. D.*	5.00
_____ HELPING YOURSELF WITH APPLIED PSYCHOLOGY *R. Henderson*	2.00
_____ HELPING YOURSELF WITH PSYCHIATRY *Frank S. Caprio, M.D.*	2.00
_____ HOW TO ATTRACT GOOD LUCK *A. H. Z. Carr*	4.00
_____ HOW TO CONTROL YOUR DESTINY *Norvell*	3.00
_____ HOW TO DEVELOP A WINNING PERSONALITY *Martin Panzer*	5.00
_____ HOW TO DEVELOP AN EXCEPTIONAL MEMORY *Young & Gibson*	4.00
_____ HOW TO OVERCOME YOUR FEARS *M. P. Leahy, M.D.*	3.00
_____ HOW YOU CAN HAVE CONFIDENCE AND POWER *Les Giblin*	3.00
_____ HUMAN PROBLEMS & HOW TO SOLVE THEM *Dr. Donald Curtis*	4.00
_____ I CAN *Ben Sweetland*	5.00
_____ I WILL *Ben Sweetland*	3.00
_____ LEFT-HANDED PEOPLE *Michael Barsley*	4.00
_____ MAGIC IN YOUR MIND *U. S. Andersen*	5.00

___ MAGIC OF THINKING BIG *Dr. David J. Schwartz*		3.00
___ MAGIC POWER OF YOUR MIND *Walter M. Germain*		5.00
___ MENTAL POWER THROUGH SLEEP SUGGESTION *Melvin Powers*		3.00
___ NEW GUIDE TO RATIONAL LIVING *Albert Ellis, Ph.D. & R. Harper, Ph.D.*		3.00
___ OUR TROUBLED SELVES *Dr. Allan Fromme*		3.00
___ PSYCHO-CYBERNETICS *Maxwell Maltz, M.D.*		3.00
___ SCIENCE OF MIND IN DAILY LIVING *Dr. Donald Curtis*		5.00
___ SECRET OF SECRETS *U. S. Andersen*		5.00
___ SECRET POWER OF THE PYRAMIDS *U. S. Andersen*		5.00
___ STUTTERING AND WHAT YOU CAN DO ABOUT IT *W. Johnson, Ph.D.*		2.50
___ SUCCESS-CYBERNETICS *U. S. Andersen*		5.00
___ 10 DAYS TO A GREAT NEW LIFE *William E. Edwards*		3.00
___ THINK AND GROW RICH *Napoleon Hill*		3.00
___ THINK YOUR WAY TO SUCCESS *Dr. Lew Losoncy*		5.00
___ THREE MAGIC WORDS *U. S. Andersen*		5.00
___ TREASURY OF COMFORT *edited by Rabbi Sidney Greenberg*		5.00
___ TREASURY OF THE ART OF LIVING *Sidney S. Greenberg*		5.00
___ YOU ARE NOT THE TARGET *Laura Huxley*		4.00
___ YOUR SUBCONSCIOUS POWER *Charles M. Simmons*		5.00
___ YOUR THOUGHTS CAN CHANGE YOUR LIFE *Dr. Donald Curtis*		5.00

SPORTS

___ BICYCLING FOR FUN AND GOOD HEALTH *Kenneth E. Luther*		2.00
___ BILLIARDS—Pocket • Carom • Three Cushion *Clive Cottingham, Jr.*		3.00
___ CAMPING-OUT 101 Ideas & Activities *Bruno Knobel*		2.00
___ COMPLETE GUIDE TO FISHING *Vlad Evanoff*		2.00
___ HOW TO IMPROVE YOUR RACQUETBALL *Lubarsky Kaufman & Scagnetti*		3.00
___ HOW TO WIN AT POCKET BILLIARDS *Edward D. Knuchell*		4.00
___ JOY OF WALKING *Jack Scagnetti*		3.00
___ LEARNING & TEACHING SOCCER SKILLS *Eric Worthington*		3.00
___ MOTORCYCLING FOR BEGINNERS *I. G. Edmonds*		3.00
___ RACQUETBALL FOR WOMEN *Toni Hudson, Jack Scagnetti & Vince Rondone*		3.00
___ RACQUETBALL MADE EASY *Steve Lubarsky, Rod Delson & Jack Scagnetti*		3.00
___ SECRET OF BOWLING STRIKES *Dawson Taylor*		3.00
___ SECRET OF PERFECT PUTTING *Horton Smith & Dawson Taylor*		3.00
___ SOCCER—The Game & How to Play It *Gary Rosenthal*		3.00
___ STARTING SOCCER *Edward F. Dolan, Jr.*		3.00
___ TABLE TENNIS MADE EASY *Johnny Leach*		2.00

TENNIS LOVERS' LIBRARY

___ BEGINNER'S BUIDE TO WINNING TENNIS *Helen Hull Jacobs*		2.00
___ HOW TO BEAT BETTER TENNIS PLAYERS *Loring Fiske*		4.00
___ HOW TO IMPROVE YOUR TENNIS—Style, Strategy & Analysis *C. Wilson*		2.00
___ INSIDE TENNIS—Techniques of Winning *Jim Leighton*		3.00
___ PLAY TENNIS WITH ROSEWALL *Ken Rosewall*		2.00
___ PSYCH YOURSELF TO BETTER TENNIS *Dr. Walter A. Luszki*		2.00
___ SUCCESSFUL TENNIS *Neale Fraser*		2.00
___ TENNIS FOR BEGINNERS, *Dr. H. A. Murray*		2.00
___ TENNIS MADE EASY *Joel Brecheen*		3.00
___ WEEKEND TENNIS—How to Have Fun & Win at the Same Time *Bill Talbert*		3.00
___ WINNING WITH PERCENTAGE TENNIS—Smart Strategy *Jack Lowe*		2.00

WILSHIRE PET LIBRARY

___ DOG OBEDIENCE TRAINING *Gust Kessopulos*		4.00
___ DOG TRAINING MADE EASY & FUN *John W. Kellogg*		4.00
___ HOW TO BRING UP YOUR PET DOG *Kurt Unkelbach*		2.00
___ HOW TO RAISE & TRAIN YOUR PUPPY *Jeff Griffen*		3.00
___ PIGEONS: HOW TO RAISE & TRAIN THEM *William H. Allen, Jr.*		2.00

The books listed above can be obtained from your book dealer or directly from Melvin Powers. When ordering, please remit 50¢ per book postage & handling. Send for our free illustrated catalog of self-improvement books.

Melvin Powers
12015 Sherman Road, No. Hollywood, California 91605

NOTES